FROGMAN

FROGMAN

COMMANDER CRABB'S STORY

BY *Marshall Pugh*

Charles Scribner's Sons

NEW YORK

FOREWORD

WHEN Commander Crabb left the Navy in the spring of 1955, we began to work together on an account of his career. It was a slow job, for whenever I pressed him for information which would show him in a brave or generous light, he would break off, abruptly remember that he had another appointment or suggest that we should take my daughter for a walk. Crabb liked to talk about his comrades and about the Italian frogmen who were technically his enemies and who later became his friends. He was never wholly convinced that there was much need to talk about himself.

Fortunately, there were many others who appreciated the work which Crabb had done, and I should like to thank them, particularly Lieutenant Joseph Howard, R.N.V.R., M.B.E., who first suggested that the book should be written; Chief Petty Officer Ralph Thorpe, Petty Officer David Bell, G.M., and Leading Stoker Sydney Knowles, B.E.M., of the Underwater

7

Working Party; and Prince Junio Valerio Borghese for his personal help and permission to draw from his book *The Sea Devils*.

Commander Crabb disappeared in Portsmouth Harbour on April 19th 1956. He was generally presumed to have died on a most dangerous underwater assignment, and since that day hundreds of thousands of words have been woven round his name. The last dive is discussed in the last chapter of this book. My hope is that the earlier chapters will provide something of the measure of the man.

MARSHALL PUGH

CONTENTS

CONTENTS

10

FROGMAN

KNOW
YOUR ENEMY

In December 1941, when the Italians had five battle-ships in the Mediterranean, the British were reduced to two, the *Valiant* and the *Queen Elizabeth,* which lay behind mine-fields and torpedo nets in the inner harbour of Alexandria. At 3.30 on the morning of 19th December, two Italians were discovered clinging to the anchor buoy at the bows of the *Valiant.* They were taken ashore for interrogation, and handed over the papers which identified them as Lieutenant de La Penne and Petty Officer Bianchi of the Italian Navy. They declined to give any more information, and were escorted back to the *Valiant* and held below-decks between the two forward gun turrets. Lieutenant de La Penne remained silent, refusing to be drawn by gibes about the Italian

13

Navy, until 5.45. Then he asked to be taken to Captain Charles Morgan of the *Valiant*. He said that the battle-ship was about to blow up, that there was nothing Captain Morgan could do about it, but that he still had time to get his men to safety if he chose. The crew were ordered on deck, the watertight doors of the *Valiant* were closed. Shortly after six there was an explosion, the battleship reared and the lights went out. The *Valiant* was temporarily out of the war.

The *Queen Elizabeth*, lying astern, rose in the water as a second explosion wrecked and flooded her boiler-rooms. A third explosion blew the stern and the propellers from a naval tanker.

In one night six men had swung the balance of sea power in the Mediterranean. They drew a tribute from Churchill to their 'extraordinary courage and ingenuity.'

'Thus,' he said, 'we no longer had any battle squadron in the Mediterranean. . . . The sea defences of the Nile Valley had to be confined to our submarine and de-stroyer flotillas, with a few cruisers and, of course, shore-based air forces. For this reason it was necessary to transfer a part of our shore-based torpedo-carrying aircraft from the south and east coast of England, where they would soon be needed, to the North African shore.'

This victory of six men was not exploited by the Italian Navy as a whole, but it inspired the Tenth Light Flotilla, whose triumph it was.

14

The Tenth Light Flotilla of the Italian Navy recruited from all three fighting Services and trained their men in two groups.

The Gamma or swimming group wore flexible rubber suits, breathing gear and swimfins. In early training they sometimes marched in Indian file along the sea bed in full war kit. They learned to swim for miles, towing small mines of neutral buoyancy. Once trained, they attached their mines with delayed-action fuses well below the waterline of Allied ships.

The second group manned piloted torpedoes, 14 feet in length, with detachable warheads or explosive noses holding 300 kilogrammes of explosive. The torpedo was normally launched from a parent submarine. A pilot sat astride it with a diver behind him. The torpedo travelled to the target ship, the diver left his seat, disconnected the warhead and attached it beneath the target with its time-fuse set.

At full speed ahead the machine moved no faster than a walking man. It turned and dived so clumsily that the operators called it 'the pig'. And yet, astride the pigs, they penetrated guarded British harbours in the Mediterranean, making a mockery of torpedo nets and barbed entanglements, of radar and echo-sounders.

Before the attack on Alexandria Prince Junio Valerio Borghese, in command of the submarine *Scirè*, had already made three piloted torpedo assaults on Gibraltar. In October 1940 he passed through the Straits of

15

Gibraltar, turned into the Bay of Algeciras, ran its length submerged and then dispatched three piloted torpedoes from the head of the Bay. Two had to be scuttled, but their crews swam to the shores of Spain, were met by Italian agents and reached home. The third penetrated to the inner harbour of Gibraltar and dived within a few hundred yards of the battleship *Barham*. The diver ran out of oxygen and had to surface. The pilot steered his machine towards the battleship until it stopped, then attempted to crawl beneath the battleship, towing his torpedo behind him on a length of rope. He was defeated by exhaustion and captured with his diver.

In May 1941 Borghese returned and launched three machines from two and a half miles to the west of Gibraltar. As there were no warships to attack, the pilots set course for merchantmen in the open Roads. When the battery of Lieutenant Vesco's machine failed, Lieutenant Visintini towed Vesco's chariot behind his own as though a breakdown service were part of the night's work. At last Vesco's torpedo was scuttled in deep water, and the two men from it rode the backs of the remaining machines, as third hands. A second machine went down. The three men aboard it swam to the Spanish coast. Visintini's machine pressed on, still with three men up. The first vessel they reached was a hospital ship, the second was Swiss, the third they passed because she was too small. Visintini aimed for a storage tanker. His diver had difficulty fitting the warhead to the target, and as the others tried to help him their machine dived for the bottom. The operators swam to Spain and met Italian agents by arrangement. All six eventually reached Italy.

In September 1941 Borghese launched another three-machine attack from the *Scirè*. Two pilots set course for ships outside the harbour, one attacking the British tanker *Fiona Shell*, while another dived beneath a cargo ship. The diver of the second machine had fixed the warhead before he discovered that the victim was the captured *Pollenzo* of Genoa. He reported to his pilot; they had a conference in the water and decided not to sink an Italian ship, even a captured Italian ship. They took the warhead off, reattached it to the torpedo and journeyed on until they found the ten-thousand-ton armed British motorship *Durham*.

On the third chariot, Lieutenant Visintini passed into the inner harbour in the wake of a ship, when the nets were dropped to let her through. He attacked the naval tanker *Denby Dale*, hoping to set her alight and fire the inner harbour. He left as he had come, scuttled his torpedo as the others had been scuttled and swam with his diver for Spain. On shore, all six operators were arrested by a Spanish frontier patrol. They were released when the Spaniards were assured that they had been attacking the British, and their words were confirmed by the uproar as the *Denby Dale* broke her back, as the *Durham* and *Fiona Shell* went down in deep water.

This was the first success of the piloted torpedoes. In December the *Scirè* launched the torpedoes which put out of action the battleships at Alexandria. In the spring of 1942 Borghese was given command of all the underwater activities of the Tenth Flotilla. He was particularly interested in Gibraltar, and great preparations for piloted torpedo attacks were made. Meantime the initiative temporarily passed to swimmers of the Gamma Group.

In July the convoy assembly area of Gibraltar overflowed with ships, until some British merchantmen lay only 400 yards from 'neutral' Spanish beaches. Twelve of the Gamma Group arrived in Spain by devious routes. Six were landed by submarine at Bordeaux and came into Spain in pairs, some by lorry, some on foot across the Pyrenees. Six more signed on as merchant seaman in Italy, and outraged the captain, who was not in the plot, by deserting his ship at Barcelona. By Madrid and Cadiz they reached the marshalling area at dawn on 13th July 1942. They spent the day there, studying their targets which were only 400 yards away.

They swam out and attacked the British merchant ships *Meta, Shuma, Baron Douglas, Empire Snipe*. Then they returned to the beach, sinking their suits, swimfins and breathing gear when the job was done. Five of the swimmers returned to Italy. The others were arrested by Spanish sentries as they landed, and remained under arrest, even when the *Meta, Shuma, Baron Douglas* and *Empire Snipe* went down. They were interned in a hotel in Seville.

Another swimming attack was planned for September and five swimmers were required. Two arrived from Barcelona, 'deserters' from another Italian merchant ship. The others were chosen from the prisoners of Seville. Petty Officer Vago Giari and two others moved out from internment, while three substitute Italian internees moved in. The Spaniards, if they noticed, did not seem to mind.

In the September attack, three swimmers set out while two reserves stood by. There was little wind, the sea was smooth and the current strong. The first swimmer, the racing yachtsman Straulino, had a great distance to swim before he reached his target. He ran out of oxygen and could not dive to fix his mine. As though there were not difficulties enough, his colleagues had a jealous scene in the water. Petty Officers Vago Giari and Bruno Di Lorenzo arrived beneath the British steamer *Raven's Point* at the same time and almost collided in the water. They made silent gestures. They tried pushing. Finally Di Lorenzo surfaced, removed his breathing gear and continued the debate at the top of his voice. He protested loudly, vehemently and correctly that the ship was his. Giari decided it was tactless to disturb the British crew of the *Raven's Point*

19

in this fashion. Reckoning that his comrade was too overcome by excitement to carry out an effective attack, he held Di Lorenzo's head beneath the water to stop him arguing, then fixed his own mine. Giari swam ashore to decent obscurity while Di Lorenzo fell into a Spanish sentry's hands.

The attack had not been a great success, but the Gamma Group diversion had achieved its object. While Giari made his way back to Italy, the great plans of the Tenth Flotilla were almost mature.

The Italian tanker *Olterra* lay at Algeciras, less than four miles from Gibraltar. On the outbreak of war she had been scuttled in the Roads of Gibraltar, then re-floated and towed into the Spanish port. Her owners had intended to sell her to a Spanish line, but the British at Gibraltar made it clear that the tanker would not sail again, whatever flag she flew. In 1942, while the tanker was still interned with a guard of Spaniards on boards, Lieutenant Visintini had her converted into a depot ship for his torpedoes.

Visintini was the most famous and perhaps the boldest of the Italian torpedo pilots. Twice he had been launched against Gibraltar by submarine and once he had penetrated to the inner harbour to sink the naval tanker *Denby Dale*. But attacks launched from sub-marines were brave gambles at best. By the time the submarine arrived from Italy, the ships she had intended to sink had often already sailed from Gibraltar. An attack from a submarine had to be planned for weeks ahead, and then it depended upon the weather and the targets of one night. Having improved upon the method, Visintini no longer needed a submarine. With his torpedoes and their crews, he was in permanent residence in the *Olterra*.

He had been given the idea of a depot ship by Antonio Ramogino, an Italian designer who had demonstrated how a tanker could be made into a floating dock for piloted torpedoes and still appear to be a normal, innocent ship. Ramogino was not thinking in terms of the *Olterra;* he had not suggested that the necessary alterations could be made in full view of the enemy. From Gibraltar the superstructure of the *Olterra* could be seen with the naked eye. The designer had not anticipated working with neutral sentries on board the vessel to be deceived. Ramogino was well aware that conditions of warfare had changed since the time of the Trojan Horse. But Visintini had convinced him that the job could be done, and they had then convinced their seniors.

The Italian Ministry of Marine was not officially informed of the project. For some time the Tenth Flotilla had been allowed to make their own arrangements with Pirelli and other Italian firms of equal ingenuity and skill. For the work a large number of Italian technicians had to be smuggled into Spain, on false pretexts and with forged papers. The Italian Ministry of Foreign Affairs declined to provide all the papers, pointing out that the number of forged documents already in the service of the Tenth Flotilla was liable to bring the Ministry into disrepute. A typist in the right department of the Ministry was persuaded to adopt a more reasonable attitude. She stole the necessary forms and arranged temporary loans of the rubber stamps.

First, a base which was near, but not too near, the *Olterra* was required for Ramogino, the designer, and the ideal place was the Villa Carmela, on the high ground of Maiorga Point, close by La Linea and a mile's walk north of Gibraltar. The Villa Carmela could be seen from Gibraltar and was often admired by soldiers of the garrison. There Signor Ramogino took his bride Conchita, letting it be known that they were on an extended honeymoon and that his wife was in need of sea air. Conchita had a broad window built. When she looked beyond the cage of parakeets in the window, she had a splendid view of British ships assembling in the Bay. She called her honeymoon home the most advanced base of the Italian Navy in enemy waters.

While her husband worked on the plans for the *Olterra*, the Villa Carmela served as a base for the Italian swimming attacks in July and September of 1942. Attacking from the north, the swimmers drew British attention from Algeciras in the west.

Visintini flew from Italy to direct operations, and

boarded the *Olterra* dressed as a merchant seaman. The captain of the ship was in the plot, and his old crew was gradually replaced. From Leghorn, Visintini's technicians and assault operators arrived singly or in pairs, with genuine passports, dramatically dirty clothing and merchant seaman's papers. At Leghorn they had taken a special course in how to dress, talk and behave like merchant seaman.

The problem of Spanish sentries aboard the tanker was quickly solved. Visintini reasoned that sentries of all nations march on their stomachs. He arranged that the cook of the *Olterra* should be well supplied with food and wine. Thereafter the Spanish sentries guarded the galley aft, while conversions were made in the bows.

The Spanish port authorities were assured that the tanker must be made ready to sail away triumphantly and soon, when the war against the Allies was won. The Italians assured the Spaniards sufficiently often to have their words reported to the British across the Bay. For one thing, the *Olterra's* trimming tanks would have to be cleaned before she sailed. It was an elaborate cleaning for such a rusty old ship. In the process a water-tight hatch was cut in the bulkhead, so that the forepeak could be reached from the forward cargo hold. The forward tanks of the *Olterra* were pumped out and her bows rose out of the water. With only a sun awning between them and the Defence Security telescopes of Gibraltar, members of the crew began to 'scrape the bows'. While they scraped energetically and noisily, a four-foot door was cut in the forepeak. When the *Olterra* resumed her normal trim in the evening, the four-foot door was six feet beneath the waterline. The forepeak was partially flooded. The cargo hold abaft the forepeak remained dry, to serve as the assembly shop and maintenance workshop for piloted torpedoes. Ready for action, they would pass through the hatch in slings into the forepeak and be lowered into the water. The torpedo pilot would then trim down and pass through the door out into the Bay, travelling six feet beneath the surface, until he was clear of the port of Algeciras.

When the ship was ready, the torpedoes began to arrive, without their warheads and tail units, marked as deck pipeline for the *Olterra*. Oil drums, ostensibly for the tanker's Diesel, came with containers of breathing gear inside them. A number of large petrol drums consigned to the Italian consulate in Algeciras each had petrol in a sheath beneath the dipstick, to satisfy the curiosity of the Spaniards, but the bulk of each drum was occupied by a torpedo warhead. The drums were cloaks for daggers. Did not the tanker herself wear a false nose?

From the grounds of the British consulate at Algeciras, an excellent pair of naval binoculars on a tripod mounting seemed to stare at the *Olterra*. None of the activity was in view, but the binoculars made the Italians thoroughly uncomfortable. The stare of the British consulate became a blind stare when men from the *Olterra* stole the binoculars one night. Visintini found they were better than his own and used them in his watch on the harbour and defences of Gibraltar.

By November or December of 1942 the Italians were ready to launch major attacks against Gibraltar bolder in conception than anything in the past.

CHAPTER 1

BOLD
BIT
OF ROCK

IN NOVEMBER 1942 when Lionel Philip Kenneth Crabb was drawn into the battle against Italian frogmen, he was thirty-two years old, opposed to any form of exercise and capable of swimming only three lengths of a swimming-pool. He was to emerge from the struggle under water as a famous frogman and a minor legend of the Mediterranean war. He was to emerge still unable to swim more than three lengths of a pool without swimfins, with his deep dislike of exercise unimpaired. In November 1942 his chance of emerging at all seemed slender. In his history there is something of the history of the British at war.

Little in his past experience had prepared him for the job. Between the two wars he had drifted amiably,

26

certain that things would be all right in the end, and they usually were. In his youth he had been apprenticed to the Merchant Navy and had sailed aboard the s.s. *Bonheur,* which plied between Buenos Aires and New York. When he was about to be examined for a second mate's ticket, he left the Merchant Navy and joined Shell Eastern Petroleum in New York, with the intention of reaching the oil-fields. He ended his career in oil, selling gas from a filling station in Windgap, Pennsylvania, and went back to London to join a cousin in an advertising syndicate. As soon as the business prospered, he sold his share.

At this time he shared a flat with a friend who was addicted to drink. When his flat-mate's parents decided that their son needed a change, they paid Crabb's passage to accompany him on a journey to the China Seas. His instructions were to keep him from strong drink on the journey and to lock him in his cabin when the ship called at ports. On their way home he was much better, and Crabb dropped off at Singapore. Having liked the Chinese people he had met, he decided to stay in Singapore and learn the language. But he could not master the subtle tones and rhythms of Chinese sounds, and he began to suspect that he was tone deaf—he certainly could not sing. He packed up and returned to London.

Most of his money had gone, and he filled in with odd jobs, once earning two guineas modelling trunks for an advertising photographer. He thought the whole thing undignified and kept his hat on to maintain his self-respect while the photographs were taken. Then, with an acquaintance who specialised in getting finance for worth-while inventions, he formed a partnership.

His partner believed that there was a great future in the work of a French inventor named de Corlieu, who had devised a pair of rubber swimfins or flippers which would allow a swimmer to balance in the water like a fish and would greatly increase his speed and power. Crabb could see no future whatever in swimfins, but he agreed to attend a demonstration of the invention in the Marshall Street baths. He was bored by the sight of a grown woman splashing about in the water, looking like an anxious seal, and when it was suggested that he should try the swimfins he excused himself and slipped quietly away.

The men with money shared his indifference to swim-fins, but they were interested in a revolutionary method of sewing kapok, which his partner and he promoted. From the proceeds Crabb made another trip to Singapore, intending to try his hand at writing Chinese characters. He returned, defeated, to London in 1938. He had an idea that a war was coming on, and he had wanted to join the Royal Navy off and on from his eighth birthday. So he approached the Royal Naval Volunteer Reserve, but they considered him too old at twenty-eight for their immediate requirements. He dropped into the Cavendish Hotel for a drink one day and stayed for a year. The Cavendish was then the most wildly exclusive hotel in London. He got on well with Rosa Lewis, the proprietress, who let him have a room on the top floor back, while he searched for a job to keep him going until the war. In the front parlour of the Cavendish he met a dealer who agreed to take him on in a gallery of modern art. There the patrons preferred to talk themselves into buying pictures, and his task was to listen to them, agreeing with them a good deal. On the whole his duties were light, and he spent his evenings studying naval gunnery. One night in 1939 he had his first underwater adventure. On his way home from the Marquis of Granby, he fell from a launch into the River Thames and he was pulled out, downstream, still holding grimly to his hat.

When war broke out the Royal Naval Volunteer Reserve still considered that Crabb was too old, and he sailed from Thameshaven as a merchant seaman gunner on a tanker for Aruba at the beginning of September 1939. A year passed before he was able to transfer to the Royal Naval Patrol Service. At Lowestoft, civilians who mustered with him and who had 'mucked about in yachts' became petty officers while he was allowed to become an able seaman. He sailed in trawlers with strange skippers and fishermen who did not care to wear naval uniform or attend divisions and who were certain that they had some special dispensation from the Articles of War.

By then, Crabb was becoming alarmed. He was accustomed to the idea that things just happened to him in peacetime, but he did not want his war to become another hilarious outing. At the end of 1941 he was commissioned. The Navy then discovered that he had a weakness in his left eye and debarred him from further sea service. Volunteering for special duties, he was appointed drainage and passive defence officer of the Coastal Forces Base at Dover. A saloon-bar acquaintance helped him to join Mine and Bomb Disposal. It would mean dangerous work, possibly in dealing with unexploded land mines in the rubble of London or in rendering charges safe on invasion beach-heads, but it was the only way he knew of getting back to service.

He did not expect to be a good disposal officer. He could not follow the theory of electricity, and at H.M.S. Volcano, the bomb-disposal school in Cumberland, he could not absorb all the details of enemy bombs. After a fortnight's course in conventional mines, he went to Swansea for experience. Long before he came Swansea had been badly beaten about, but there were no longer land mines or unexploded bombs for his attention. From the time he arrived, he was involved in a bitter struggle with the local naval padre who wanted to employ the Swansea Bomb-disposal Party in the grounds of the officers' club. It all fitted too neatly into the pattern of Crabb's previous experience and he could no longer enjoy the joke.

In November 1942 he sailed for Gibraltar to take up duties there as mine and bomb-disposal officer. All he knew of Gibraltar was that it was a bold bit of rock, a British stronghold guarding the western approaches to the Mediterranean. Otherwise he expected Gibraltar to be as dull as Swansea—a dismal depot ship for distant wars. When he disembarked he did not know that Italian frogmen were attacking shipping at Gibraltar; he had never heard of Italian frogmen. He walked up to the Tower to report to Commander Ralph Hancock, who was in command of minesweeping and extended defence. Commander Hancock quickly corrected his notions of the job.

The Commander detailed the Italian underwater attacks upon Gibraltar. Outside, the U-boats were hunting in packs of sometimes twenty. During the last year the German Navy had sunk six million tons, losing one U-boat for every sixty thousand tons of Allied shipping they destroyed.

While Allied naval defences were stretched close to breaking point, convoys of fifty, sixty ships and sometimes more assembled in the Roads of Gibraltar and spread out towards the Spanish coast. Shipping security was impossible when almost every visiting vessel was in view of Italian and German consulates in the neighbouring Spanish ports. Hundreds of dockyard workers

31

from Spain came into Gibraltar each day from La Linea, a Spanish town which is separated from Gibraltar by a narrow strip of sand, and they left for home at curfew time each night, The ships were known to the enemy by day, and at night they did not have the shelter of the dark. Gibraltar had been lit up through the worst of the siege and so remained. To have imposed a black-out would only have served to silhouette the keep against the lights of Spain.

Within the inner harbour were warships refitting and refuelling. Outside the harbour the water was too deep for many ships to anchor and so they lay north of Gibraltar, near La Linea. Some of the ships were no more than 400 yards from Spanish beaches. From the beaches, Allied ships stretched in lines which were often three miles long from east to west. The ships in the west were close to the Spanish port of Algeciras, across the Bay of Gibraltar, and the proximity to Spain of British ships made it very much easier for Italian frogmen to harry the flanks and then to escape. The project of attacking Gibraltar themselves was one which was never far from many Spanish minds.

So far as was known, the enemy had suffered no casualties. Only two of their men had been captured. There were easy pickings in the Roads of Gibraltar.

Three British naval harbour defence launches patrolled the ships at anchor in the Roads and systematically dropped light depth-charges in the water. The launches ran round all night, sweeping the water and the sides of ships with their lights. Three launches could not guard all ships at all times in the great lake of night, but a larger defence force could not be spared.

During Italian attacks, British naval divers searched the bottoms of ships in the likely areas for mines and warheads. If they found any charges and if they managed to take them off before they exploded, it would be Lieutenant Crabb's job as mine-disposal officer to render the charges safe on land.

'I see,' Crabb said. He temporarily lost track of the Commander's words while he thought about the job the naval clearance divers were expected to do. They were to search the bottoms of ships, in deep water and all weathers in the dark. They had to choose 'likely areas' where they could begin to search . . . likely areas among an assembly of ships three miles long and a mile across. He remembered his own experience in deep water, when he had fallen into the Thames, tried to swim and had been dragged down by the ebb tide. By all accounts there was some fast water at Gibraltar. Even if a diver found the right ship, he might be beneath it when a torpedo warhead exploded. Obviously the divers of Gibraltar were a large, *élite*, highly trained team of powerful swimmers. He certainly did not envy them their job.

'How many divers are there?' he asked.

'Two,' said Hancock. 'They are not professional divers,

33

they are not mine-disposal people and they have no proper diving-gear.'

It occurred to Crabb that he ought to volunteer to join the divers. They were strong swimmers apparently, and he was a weak swimmer. But he was mine-disposal officer and it could be argued that, if the mines were under water, the mine-disposal officer should have to do his job.

He decided that the best thing to do was to make up his mind quickly. On the afternoon of his arrival, he went to see the diving officer, Lieutenant William Bailey, and asked if he wanted a hand. His voice was deep and his words were measured. He said nothing about his shortcomings as a swimmer. Crabb was under medium height, with a superbly bold, aggressive, sharpened nose. Hair grew high on his cheeks and his curling beard was rich and red. It was not a growth hurriedly raised for the Volunteer Reserve; it had earned him the nickname 'Admiral' years before the war. He looked a most resolute officer.

'Crabb . . .' said Bailey, 'a fine name for this job.' He explained that they had no diving-gear to compare with the equipment of the enemy . . . jolly hard lines, but there it was. Since they had no rubber suits, they dived day and night in swimming-trunks, and it really was extraordinary how quickly one got used to it, just like the swimmers in the Serpentine. Bailey had borrowed sixteen Davis Submerged Escape Apparatus sets from a submarine depot ship. The DSEA set was intended to help submariners to escape from a submarine. It was neither intended nor in any way suitable for operational diving, but it was better than trying to dive on a deep breath. Neither Bailey nor his assistant, Leading Seaman Bell, knew how to service the sets properly. Leading Seaman Bell had invented his own diving helmet from a football bladder which he had sealed at the neck and fitted with goggles from an old gas-mask. Bailey didn't advise Crabb to try it; he didn't think that Bell had much future as a designer.

Now that Crabb was in the picture, would he like to try a dip? He dressed in naval overalls and gym shoes. Bailey showed him how to strap on the DSEA set, how to hold the mouthpiece and how to breathe. He put on a pair of goggles which did not fit too well and he felt most unpleasantly conspicuous. Bailey led him to the edge of the quay, tied a string round his wrist and told him that the object of the exercise was to walk down and up a ladder into twelve feet of water, practising breathing.

As he struggled down the ladder, he was not certain whether he was breathing properly. He climbed down the ladder, up again, surfaced, then tried the drill again. He did not go to the bottom of the ladder for he had heard that small octopuses gathered in the depth beneath the quay, and he hated the very thought of

35

octopuses, they reminded him of worms. The rope at his
wrist tightened and then tugged. He was wanted on the
surface.

'Sorry about this,' Bailey said; 'had to bring you back.
Enjoy your dip? I have to go. There's a flap on in the
harbour. Mines have been reported.' But Crabb understood the drill now, didn't he? He didn't need a piece of
string any more, did he? There wasn't much to it, was
there? Piece of cake. He suggested that his pupil should
carry on practising alone, and Crabb obeyed.

Bailey had been called on a false alarm and he soon
returned to suggest that if Crabb felt that he was quite
happy about the gear, he would show him how to
examine a ship. They went out in the diving-launch to
a ship which was drawing about twelve feet of water.
From the ship a bottom line depended and they dived
together from the ship, heading for the line. Crabb was
aware that the water was very blue and clear, the
blue of deep water over a rock-and-sand bottom, under
a clear sky. He saw that the hull of the ship was red,
and then he was much too anxious and involved to
notice anything more. They pulled themselves down
the line and grasped the bilge-keel ledge of the ship,
running along well beneath the waterline, like a narrow
metal ruler. The divers pulled themselves along it
towards the stern, examining for mines. Crabb had
great difficulty in staying on. The swell was such that
they were often wrenched from their holds. He was

afraid of deep water but a little more afraid of displaying his fear.

The gym shoes that they wore were weighted so that they could remain upright under water. In Gibraltar, in 1942, no one knew that a diver could weight his belt to remain upright and still leave his feet free. At the end of the bilge-keel they surfaced and swam upright with a laboured dead-foot breast stroke, to examine the rudders and propellers of the ship, before boarding the diving-launch tied up astern. On the far side of the ship they completed the examination of the bilge-keel, and the pupil was thoroughly exhausted.

When they returned to the shore, Bailey officially accepted Crabb as a member of the clearance diving team. They dried themselves, dressed and drank to a successful partnership. Crabb tried to draw the other out on the Italian underwater mines that he had found, but Bailey made it sound a rather dull aquatic sport and soon changed the subject. After he had gone, Crabb made a few enquiries. He discovered that Bailey was officially Electrical Officer of a minesweeping flotilla, and he had taken on the diving job because there appeared to be no other officer immediately available or suitable for it. He was a keen swimmer; he had once taken a short course in conventional mines, and his most hair-raising exploit had followed the first Italian swimming attack on Gibraltar in July 1942.

A large party of Italian saboteurs had swum under

cover of darkness, probably from the beaches close to
La Linea, with mines which could be held up under
ships by inflated rubber rings. They had placed their
mines with delayed-action fuses set and had returned,
undetected, to Spain. In the morning the explosions
began. Bailey, with Leading Seaman Bell, had gone
diving under ships in search of mines which were about
to explode. They had found a number of them, and
Bailey had slashed at the rubber rings which held them,
puncturing the rings and sending the mines tumbling
into deep water to explode at their leisure. Considering
the action and the way Bailey had described it, Crabb
realized that Bailey was his master in the calculated
understatement. It was not easy to out-English Crabb.

A British agent at Huelva reported that a new type
of mine had been washed ashore on a beach near the
Spanish port. It was a limpet mine, to be towed by a
swimmer, and it was more complicated than those which
Bailey had destroyed like pricked balloons. The new
weapon was designed to be clamped directly to the
bilge-keel of a ship and to hang on while the ship was
under way. It could be set not to explode for many hours
after it had been placed.

No more detail of the mine was available, but its use
was obvious. Italian saboteurs, probably operating from
Italian ships in Spanish harbours, intended to sabotage
British merchant ships which called at the ports. From
their own ship they might have no more than a few yards

to swim under water to fix the limpet to the bilge keel
of a British ship. To sink British ships directly in neutral
harbours would cause the Italians and the Spaniards a
certain amount of diplomatic embarrassment. So the
mine was designed to hang on while the ship was under
way, and was given a delayed-action fuse which would
fire the mine when the ship was many hours at sea. The
ship would go down, apparently torpedoed.

All merchant ships using Spanish ports were warned,
and as they arrived from Spain to join a convoy at Gibraltar they were examined by divers.

The mine could be set so that the ship would carry
it back to Gibraltar, then blow up at anchor there. The
method would be easier to discover, but it would
establish that the sinking was an Italian job and not
the work of a German submarine. Besides, it would be
a more theatrical sinking. It had long been obvious
that the underwater saboteurs of the Italian Tenth
Flotilla had leanings towards drama. From the day the
mine was reported, Bailey or Bell dived under every
British ship arriving from Spain.

Each day Crabb dived with them, slowly gaining confidence in himself and in his gear. To his surprise he
found that he was beginning to enjoy the sensation of
diving, despite his breathing gear, his poor swimming
and the cold. Under water on a clear day he could see
for almost sixty feet around him, and he began to wish
that he could name the plants and fish that he saw. He

felt that if he had a solid month of steady training, he might be able to deal with an underwater mine, alone.

When Bailey tripped on his way downstairs and broke an ankle, Crabb was temporarily made diving officer. He had made his first dive in the last week of November. On 4th December he found his first limpet mine.

CHAPTER 2

THE
GREEN MINE

THE STEAMER *Willowdale* came in from Huelva, with wolfram valued at £250,000. The *Willowdale* was old to be abroad in such dangerous waters, and moreover burdened by her 1200 tons. When she was moored Crabb came alongside in the diving-launch. Leading Seaman Bell was with him, but he chose to take the first inspection-dive. He worked his way along the bilge keel and saw something hanging on it, close by the engine-room. He looked again, he blinked and looked for a third time. His goggles did not fit properly and they were flooding, while the swell threatened to take him off the bilge keel. He gripped a little tighter and had another look.

The mine on the bilge keel of the *Willowdale* was

41

about three feet long, torpedo-shaped and green; attached to the ship by three clamps. It was much larger than the floating mines that Bailey and Bell had described. He had not seen such a mine before, either in a book or in a demonstration room.

His goggles continued flooding. At one moment they were clear, the next water danced in them as in an eye-bath, and the mine danced with it. At one moment the mine was squat, then it was tall, then long, and then it curved like a boomerang. As he broke surface, he noticed that, for the first time in his week of diving, he had found it easy to breathe. The mine had taken his mind off the shortcomings of his apparatus.

Lieutenant Crabb climbed aboard the steamer and he asked her captain to get the engine-room evacuated and to move all the hands forward, away from the mine. The mate stayed astern and warmed the divers with some rum. Leading Seaman Bell was ordered to stay in the launch, for the Director of Bomb Disposal had ruled that no rating should ever touch a live enemy mine or bomb. Ratings might help to search for mines but they were not allowed to move one or attempt to render it safe.

Crabb dived alone and began to wrestle with the first clamp. The mine had been fixed, then tightened with a clockwise twist of the clamps. There was a fair chance that the anti-clockwise twist to slacken the clamps might bring a booby-trap into play. Normally a mine would be fired by time-clocks, somewhere inside. The ship had made a day's run from Huelva, where the mine must have been placed by saboteurs, and the time for the clocks to strike must be growing near. There was an unusual mechanism at the tail of this mine. Crabb had no way of understanding the mine until he had it on land. As he struggled with the first clamp, as he tried to twist it anti-clockwise, he also tried to disregard the various unpleasant possibilities.

All that he could imagine was a nervous flash. He tried to persuade himself that the mine would not explode to spite him. He had an excellent chance of surviving. He wanted to pray and he could not think who the saint of underwater work might be. He settled for St. Nicholas. Then he wondered how much physical pain an explosion would cause.

The first clamp slackened.

He began to work on the second and it slackened. It seemed unlikely on the odds that the third clamp would be booby-trapped. The third clamp turned a little and then it stuck. As he began to wrestle and jerk, he no longer considered that the odds were so much in his favour. He breathed in pure oxygen and exhaled into his breathing-bag CO_2, which was absorbed by a canister of soda lime. The moment breathing became uncomfortable he turned the valve of his oxygen bottle and more oxygen hissed into the bag. When the first oxygen bottle was exhausted, he surfaced for a fresh supply and dived to attack the clamp again. While the clamp stayed firm, his second oxygen bottle was exhausted. As he surfaced for a third supply, he stored up memories of the coloured, noisy, normal things above the water. He was shivering in his swimming trunks, his hands were numb and he wanted a cigarette badly. Bell and the mate had just lit cigarettes and he refused a third light from the first match. Crabb was highly superstitious. He lit his own cigarette with a fresh light and made sure that the match he held was steady. Leading Seaman Bell wanted to talk to him alone. Bell was embarrassed. 'Can I have a go, sir?' he asked. He would not have liked anyone to see him volunteering like that to an officer, it would have 'looked like he was all for it'.

Crabb remembered the ruling of the Director of Bomb Disposal, with which he entirely agreed. But the mine had to come off, and he was very nearly beaten. He let Bell try. Waiting for Bell to reappear was much worse than dealing with the mine. Bell surfaced, flushed with the effort of breathing and struggling under water. He had had no luck, and Crabb dived again. The water still danced in his goggles, the swell still threatened to wrench him off his hold, his resistance was weakening and he wondered how long it had been since he began work on the third clamp. Without warning, the clamp slackened in his hands. He flinched, but the mine was not booby-trapped.

44

Technicalities which had seemed difficult when he was learning the drills of mine disposal became quite clear. The mine might be fitted with hydrostatic switches and might explode at a change of water pressure, if he took it up to the surface. Of neutral buoyancy, it floated where he had found it, and he moored it at the same depth, beneath two buoys.

Then he boarded the launch and sat, dripping water, for some time. He had struggled with the mine for three-quarters of an hour. Having rested, he had to tow the buoys with the mine beneath them, until he reached a mooring rock in Rosia Bay, a quiet inlet almost at Europa Point. By the time he had moored the buoys it was too late to do anything more that night. He rowed back to report to Commander Hancock. He was looking forward to a hot bath and a meal. There was a fair chance that the mine would blow, harmlessly, at its new mooring. If it didn't, he would deal with it in the morning.

In the morning the mine was still there. 'The next problem,' said Commander Hancock, 'is where are we going to unbutton this thing? With the war and one thing and another, there really isn't a great deal of space for experimental work of this kind. The place is rather congested.'

Hancock chose a deserted spot on the edge of the airstrip which runs from beach to beach across the narrow neck joining Gibraltar to the Spanish mainland. The mine was towed behind a rowing-boat beneath the buoys. When they landed Crabb was to pull the mine, inch by inch, ashore on a long line and to stand far enough away to escape injury if it exploded. But the chosen spot, they found, was heavily wired off and could not be used. There remained only the runway itself, congested with Spitfires standing almost wing-tip to wing-tip. Hancock, confident that they could strip the new mine safely, said that they would have to do their work between two Spitfires. He felt it would be wiser on the whole not to inform the Royal Air Force of his plan and so spread alarm and despondency.

Clearly, the mine could not be dragged between Spitfires on a long line; there was no margin for error. Crabb had to drag the mine into the shallows, then lift it ashore, cradling the twenty-five-pound mine in his arms like a baby.

As senior officer and a torpedo officer at that, the Commander insisted that he should help in stripping the mine, and Crabb watched him anxiously as he arrogantly wielded his spanner. The junior officer would have preferred to do all the spanner work himself; other people in the neighbourhood of a mine made him nervous.

They examined the unusual tailpropeller mechanism of the mine and found it ingenious. When the *Willowdale* had left Huelva with the mine on her bilge keel, the propeller in the tail of the mine had begun to turn.

After so many revolutions it would have actuated a detonator which would have fired the mine.

This propeller mechanism was only a secondary means of firing the mine. Inside the shell were three time-clocks set to fire the explosive after the ship had been a certain number of hours away from Huelva. They stripped it and removed the clocks. Three detonators, each the length of the cap of a pen and the thickness of a pen, were removed without further delay. Then Hancock went off with the clocks to show them to the Admiral, Sir Frederick Edward-Collins. When he had gone, Crabb cleared up. He found that two of the three detonators were missing, and out of their environment such detonators were particularly sensitive. He began to search around.

Just before he was about to admit defeat, a messenger arrived to summon him to lunch with the Governor. Commander Hancock was already in attendance, for the Governor wanted full details of the mine, with its proof of sabotage from neutral ports, immediately. It had been a wearing morning: while he answered questions, Lieutenant Crabb could have been excused for having forgotten about the detonators. It had been an equally wearing morning for Commander Hancock, who had the detonators loose in his pocket throughout the lunch.

Ralph Hancock had other things on his mind. The mine on the *Willowdale* had been an unpleasant reminder that the Tenth Light Flotilla had not lost interest in his parish. It would have been a simple matter for the Italians to set the clocks to fire the mine long before the *Willowdale* reached Gibraltar. No piloted torpedoes had been launched into the Bay of Algeciras for more than a year. The Tenth Flotilla was not usually slow to exploit a successful method of attack. It was possible that something big was brewing.

CHAPTER 3

DIVE
IN THE DARK

THE MORNING of 5th December 1942 had also been a wearing one for Lieutenant Visintini of the Italian Navy in his depot ship *Olterra* at Algeciras. He had spent it in checking his piloted torpedoes and in briefing their crews. In his spare moments in daytime he had studied the defences of Gibraltar, using the pair of binoculars stolen from the British consulate at Algeciras.

At night he had absorbed the procedure of the British patrol boats and listened while they systematically dropped light depth-charges. By November, when Crabb arrived in Gibraltar, Visintini had an exact plan for dodging the patrol boats and entering the inner harbour. He could see that the entrances were guarded by four strange shore-based mortars which fired small

49

depth-charges into the entrances at intervals through the night. He calculated that he could slip through between shots.

He expected a diversion not unlike the swimming attacks of the summer. Italian sabotage parties were assembling at Malaga, Huelva, Cadiz, Barcelona, Oporto. Diving from Italian ships in the ports, frogmen would fit delayed-action mines beneath British merchant ships. When merchant ships arrived at Gibraltar and suddenly went down in daylight the British would be fully occupied.

On 6th December Visintini saw Force H enter harbour, with the battleship *Nelson* and the aircraft carriers *Furious* and *Formidable,* and in his diary he wrote a message for his wife:

Last night, when I told you we were on the eve of an important event, I told the truth without realising it, for, in view of the arrival of the British squadron, I have decided to take action tomorrow night. . . .

He added:

And if God wills to protect us, our success, alone, will be an eloquent reply to the facile and barbarous triumphs of the haughty British power.

We, the pygmies, are resolved to strike you boldly to the heart, in the fleet which is your greatest pride. And we expect that this gesture of ours will cause the world to realise, once and for all, what stuff we Italians are made of.

Visintini decided to attack the *Nelson* himself while the two other pilots under his command attacked the

Formidable and the *Furious*. His old comrade Lieutenant de La Penne had sunk two battleships at Alexandria. Visintini, also, intended to sally forth and alter the course of a war.

The Gibraltar bomb-disposal party had prepared charges for the shore-based mortars which Visintini had seen. On the morning of 7th December they were hard at work preparing more. They had a large number of tins with fuses attached to them, which were often optimistically described as depth-charge containers. They filled each tin with a pound and a quarter of TNT, fitted the pickle-bottle-type lids to the tins, then filed the more awkward edges of the lids. A civilian armament supply official protested when the filing began. He said that he was most unhappy to see spark flying from tins filled with TNT with their fuses in place. Couldn't the edges be filed before the tins were filled?

Crabb explained that this would make the work slower. The fuses of the tins were taped down and there was little likelihood of a spark from the filing setting a fuse alight. The civilian was not convinced. He pointed out that sparks were flying around in the neighbourhood of other fuses, detonators, large quantities of explosives. He looked suspiciously at the bearded Crabb as though suspecting a Gunpowder Plot.

To keep him happy, Crabb ordered his men to keep down sparks by *wetting* their files. It was true that the charges had to be prepared in great haste. He had been told that if Italian piloted torpedoes were to attack at all that month, they would attack soon, while the moon was feeble. A young moon was a torpedo moon.

There were two wide entrances to the harbour, guarded after dusk by a light broad pattern of wire and by a torpedo net. The defence had originally been designed to hold out submarines and conventional torpedoes. It had been proved that it could not contain a determined torpedo pilot. But Operation Torch, the Allied invasion of French North Africa, had begun in November. The British Navy was fighting for the whole of the North African shore and could spare no men, ships or materials to bolster the defences of Gibraltar.

In the new moon of December, four transports with United States troops for Operation Torch were anchored before the moles at the northern entrance, in the special anchorage for very valuable ships. In the inner harbour were *Nelson, Formidable, Furious,* ammunition ships, naval tankers, submarines—a plump Armada for the fire ships.

The active defence of the entrance depended upon the four weird weapons for which Crabb was preparing ammunition. They were mounted on the knuckles of the moles, two at the north entrance and two at the south. They were known as modified Northover projectors, and they might have been described in Visintini's words as 'facile and barbarous triumphs.' The projector's were lengths of boiler tubing mounted on wooden supports. They looked like cannons run up by a studio property department for a low-budget pirate film. The projectors were the standing joke of Gibraltar. The Flag Officer of Force H had taken two to Algiers, and on passage he had temporarily mounted them on his quarter-deck behind the *Nelson's* mighty guns and called them his secondary armament.

When firing, the gunner chose a 'depth-charge' tin which was not too ill-shapen, and put it into the barrel of the projector. At the other end of the barrel he had the firing mechanism of an ordinary rifle. Fitting a ballistite cartridge into the breach, he closed the bolt and fired the projector by pulling a lanyard. The cartridge lit the fuse on the tin of TNT and flung it into the water. There were many complications. Some of the tins did not fit properly. After the projector had been fired, they tended to stick in the barrel, the fuse burning briskly. The orders were amended. The gunner placed the tin in the barrel, inserted the cartridge, closed the bolt and retreated behind a concrete wall, holding the end of the lanyard. He pulled the lanyard and stayed behind the wall, until he saw the spark which showed that the tin was in flight with its fuse alight. If he saw no spark, he was instructed to get down behind the concrete wall and wait. In the excitement of manning the projectors curious gunners who had seen no spark were inclined to walk up from behind cover and gaze down the barrel to see what was happening. One gunner was lost when he heard a charge fall on land and went to look for it in the dark.

In an attack, the projectors were to come under the diving officer's command. Crabb did his best to persuade the gunners to have confidence in their weapons, and he reminded them to let the patrol boats pass before they fired. During an attack, the diving officer was also to be responsible for the movements of patrol boats.

The gunners fired irregularly through every night. Their projectors were supposed to 'command' the entrances to the harbour. The entrances were 150 yards across and shelved very rapidly into deep water. The gunners did not know that a charge which fell more than thirty feet from a torpedo was unlikely to give him more than a bad shock.

But from the *Olterra* the projectors appeared very much more efficient than in fact they were. They seemed to the Italians to fire regularly with murderous monotony, and Visintini's plan was to pass into the harbour in a systematic lull between shots. It was an extremely bold plan, though so far the Italians had suffered no casualties in their attacks upon Gibraltar.

Visintini in another message for his wife had written:

I know that I shall fight with deliberate, cool and unqualified determination, because I want to feel the chains that weigh us down come loose, fall and rattle as they break. When I die, my beloved, it will be in the blaze of freedom for which we are fighting.

54

On the night of the 7th, the torpedoes were lowered in their slings into the flooded forepeak of the *Olterra*. Visintini trimmed down and cruised out through the diving door into the Bay, with his diver, Petty Officer Magro, on the seat behind him. They were followed by Midshipman Manisco and Petty Officer Varini. Sub-Lieutenant Cella with his diver, Leone, brought up the rear, and they crossed the Bay at wide intervals.

The first torpedo reached the entrance to the inner harbour. An irregular shot from the modified North-over projector must have fallen very close. The charge killed Visintini and his diver.

At 11.30 Manisco and Varini were spotted by a British sentry on the Detached Mole, as they surfaced just outside the harbour. The sentry shouted, he fired and a searchlight was brought to bear, just before the piloted torpedo dived. A patrol boat gave chase, with a bomb-disposal rating on board lighting the fuses of tins of TNT by hand and throwing them into the water. Twenty minutes later Manisco and Varini scuttled their torpedo, sank their diving-suits, then climbed aboard a United States ship to surrender. They refused to say whether or where their warhead had been placed. Somehow they preserved their presence of mind and convinced interrogators that they had been launched from the Italian submarine *Ambra*. With them, the secret of the *Olterra* was safe. While they were taken ashore, Sub-

Lieutenant Cella was heading back across the Bay for the *Olterra*, at full speed. Somewhere on the way, Diver Leone fell off and drowned.

Meanwhile patrol boats and projectors continued to fire, sometimes at shadows. No one knew how many torpedoes had attacked or how many warheads had been placed. A projector gunner had claimed a hit, but no one but the gunners thought the story likely.

Commander Hancock and Lieutenant Crabb took the launch out to the first transport with its cargo of men, at about one in the morning, for the transports were the obvious place to begin searching for mines. The whole idea of searching a ship of that size seemed ludicrous. It seemed as much bigger than the *Willowdale* as Windsor Castle is larger than a villa. They climbed a weary succession of companion-ladders to the bridge. The troops on board had been alerted; they were at action stations in steel helmets and the guns were manned. As he climbed, Crabb wondered what the ship was proposing to fire upon. On the bridge, he and Hancock explained what piloted torpedoes were, what warheads were, how they were placed; they tried not to be irritated when they were disbelieved. They asked for a bottom line to be rigged. They also requested that no one should throw charges in the water while Crabb was diving. It was a dangerous request; Crabb was afraid that if the order were circulated it would merely put the idea into soldierly minds. He changed into swimming trunks, gym shoes and DSEA set in the chart-house, far above the water-line.

Within about half an hour, a bottom line was rigged. He descended to the diving-launch, had it brought round the side and struck out for the bottom line from the transport. He had a torch at his wrist, but it gave only a few inches of visibility. He grasped the bilge keel and began to work his way aft. Never having seen an Italian torpedo warhead even in daylight, he was not at all sure that he could take one off in the dark. He was more frightened still of the water intake for the engines. It was noisy and it gurgled, and he felt as if he, too, was being sucked from the sea into the engine-room.

At first, in the dark, he did not want to stray too far from the bottom line. The launch was pacing him as if he were swimming the Channel, and he would have given a great deal at that moment to have been a strong swimmer. The weighted gym shoes were dragging. Leading Seaman Bell followed him over the side; he also was diving at night for the first time.

They cleared both sides of the first transport and rested in the launch. They warmed themselves with rum and Crabb considered the orders which a staff captain had given. With one man, as totally untrained for night work as himself, he was to search the bottoms of the four transports, *then* go into the inner harbour and examine the mighty keels of the *Nelson* and the aircraft carriers. The whole job was to be completed by dawn. A fully trained, fully equipped clearance-diving team might conceivably have done the job in the time.

When dawn broke, they were still searching the last transport. If any warheads had been placed elsewhere, they would have exploded by that time. There was no point in going on. They dried themselves, drank cocoa and turned in.

No warheads or mines had been placed. For the Italians it had been an expensive night.

At nine in the morning, Crabb reported for duty. There was no clear proof that a torpedo crew had been destroyed in the entrance to the harbour, but it was known that Manisco and Varini had scuttled their craft in the Bay, not far from the harbour entrance. Charioteers were already training in Britain and it was vital that they should know more of the assault craft of the enemy. Of course, Crabb was told nothing of this. He was simply ordered to 'try' to recover the piloted torpedo in the Bay as quickly as possible. He did not suggest that this was a major salvage operation, beyond the scope of one bomb-disposal officer who was trying to improve his standard of swimming. Nor did he ask how he was supposed to tackle the job. He knew that if ships were available to detect the presence of the torpedo, with standard divers to go down to examine a strike, the Navy would have sent them.

He had to have a method of his own to find a fourteen-foot-long torpedo, lying in more than a hundred feet of water, somewhere in a bold sweep of Bay.

In the harbour was a diving-bell which had been supplied to the Admiralty about forty years before. The surface unit was a specially constructed barge, with a central well through which ran an air-lock shaft with a rectangular diving-chamber on the end of the shaft. The chamber was open-bottomed; water was kept out by air pressure. The shaft travelled down through the well until the chamber was about forty feet beneath the water, like the head of a mighty steam-hammer. The whole bell weighed about fifty tons and was entirely intended to be used in examining the moorings in the shallow peace of the inner harbour. But improvisation is the handmaid of war.

After forty years in the harbour the bell barge put out into the Bay and sent its diving-chamber down, to search deep water for the torpedo. This was its finest hour. In the chamber, down below, Crabb took a seat with the regular Spanish divers. Beneath them the water was like a sheet of glass and they could see the bottom clearly. They saw an octopus, they saw some fascinating marine plants, they saw a great deal of water, rock and sand. It was then that Crabb realised the enormousness of the job and appreciataed how small his chances were. The bell barge put out every day for more than a week and the novelty of going down the ladder of the air-lock shaft to sit in ordinary clothing beneath the sea was soon lost.

Before the barge sailed in from the Bay to the shallow waters of the harbour, the raising winches had to turn to draw the shaft up through the well, lifting the diving-chamber. Once the operation was left too late, the bell struck rock and pealed to the best of its ability. Shortly afterwards the search for the piloted torpedo was abandoned.

When Crabb returned to normal duties, a crate arrived at his office with the compliments of the Maintenance Commander. Inside was a quantity of Italian equipment which had been removed from dead men. In this fashion he was informed that his projectors had done their strange job. Two bodies had at last been recovered from the harbour entrance. He enquired about arrangements for the burial, and learned that it was merely a matter of the maintenance department getting rid of the bodies which were in the morgue. They still wore the overalls with their names: Visintini, Magro. He had never heard of them; all he knew was that they had been gallant men.

With Bailey he bought a wreath, acquired two Italian flags and asked a priest to join them aboard a tender. Visintini and Magro were buried at sea. Aboard the *Olterra* the re-forming piloted torpedo crews heard of the gesture and, in course of time, acknowledged it. The war underwater was to be a private war in which men respected their enemies.

CHAPTER 4

UNDERWATER
WORKING
PARTY

JUST before Christmas of 1942, Lieutenant Bailey was awarded the George Medal for his underwater work. Many believed that he had been decorated for diving armed with a fighting knife and slashing away at an Italian frogman's breathing gear. Bailey was sustained in dangerous work by his highly developed sense of the ridiculous. His friends regularly suffered from it.

When the award was announced, an Army battery commander who had often been Bailey's victim invited him and Crabb to his mess to celebrate. It was Christmas, after all. They arrived to find the battery commander apparently in an advanced stage of celebration. He was flushed and his words were swaying gently on their consonants. 'Bill,' he said to Bailey, 'this is a wonderful thing, your George Medal. Must think of some special way of celebrating in style.'

Gibraltar was no longer threatened by invasion from Spain. Two years and seven months had passed since General Franco had offered to enter the war, on condition that he was given Gibraltar, French Morocco and West Algeria. The tide of war in the Mediterranean was running in the Allies' favour. Yet from time to time, at a given signal, every searchlight on Gibraltar searched and every gun responded, to impress the Spaniards. This was known as Exercise Gehenna. After much drinking and rejoicing, the Army captain drew Crabb aside and said, 'Don't tell Bailey, but Exercise Gehenna is on tonight.' He spoke in a remarkably sober voice.

At ten, the captain said, 'Bill, I'll tell you what I'll do for you. I'll fire my guns.'

'Don't be a fool.'

'I insist.'

'Sit down. Have another drink.'

At 10.55 the battery commander rose again, patted Bailey's arm and staggered out into the night. At eleven, every gun in Gibraltar sounded. The bold Bailey fainted in his chair.

It was a joke in questionable taste, as many of the jokes of Gibraltar were. In the war years on the enormous lighthouse, slapstick humour was most appreciated when it verged on pandemonium. Men looked for bold relief from the tunnel-life and tedium.

When Bailey and Crabb called for diving volunteers, they were inundated with offers. From the time of Visintini's attack, it had been obvious that the naval diving party would have to expand from two officers, one of whom had a broken ankle. Leading Seaman Bell had been recalled to his ship. With an appreciation of the quiet phrase, the name Underwater Working Party was chosen, and recruiting began.

Bailey and Crabb were restricted to men who could be spared from their ships or from shore work at Gibraltar, and very few commanding officers considered that any of their men could be spared. Crabb shared a room with a troubled administrative officer who walked in his sleep; the sleep-walker most gallantly volunteered. So did many other officers involved in other work. They would be available by telephone, they said. The moment there was trouble in the harbour, they would leave their decks and turn up. They were thanked, and turned down. The Underwater Working Party had to be a proper unit.

Very few of the ratings who applied, with their commanding officers' consent, were suitable. Signalman Joseph 'Rattler' Morgan of Preston was the first man to be accepted. He was followed by Leading Torpedo Operator Jock Frazer from Glasgow, who had been a member of the shore bomb-disposal party. They were good men; they had to be. Here is how one rating diver described his early training:

63

'The morning I joined, Lieutenant Crabb, as he was then, said, "We're searching this morning. Come on out." He threw a Davis set at me. "It works like this, it works like that," he said. "Try it on." Then a little while later I was floating around a bilge keel, and that's how I started. First time I'd been under water any distance in my life. Luckily I was a good swimmer. I could do a mile any time.

'When we got to the first ship, Lieutenant Crabb said, "Follow me down this ladder and don't forget not to hold on to your breath under water as you do naturally." I followed him round the bilge keel and the stern. We got picked up in the boat, we did three or four ships more, and that was me acclimatised. Within a few days I was duty diver. I had six ships to search, and if I saw anything unusual I was to surface immediately and call for Lieutenant Crabb.'

The Party badly wanted a petty officer instructor in Davis Escape Apparatus who could train the men and the officers, but there was no such petty officer available. None could be spared from the training of submariners. After their fashion, the Party serviced their own DSEA sets. The oxygen bottles had to be renewed with a fresh supply of air, which they arranged for with flasks of oxygen and a length of copper tube with a tap. They knew that a canister on the set absorbed the carbon dioxide which they exhaled. When the set became too uncomfortable to work in, the divers concluded that the

64

Crabb (left) and Hodges after having been the first to reach the sunken submarine *Truculent* in 1950.

Crabb dives to carry out tests for the British Ministry of Agriculture and Fisheries.

When naval divers dropped to the bed of the Bay of Tobermory to search for a sunken Spanish galleon, Crabb swam round them; assisting, encouraging and clearing obstructions.

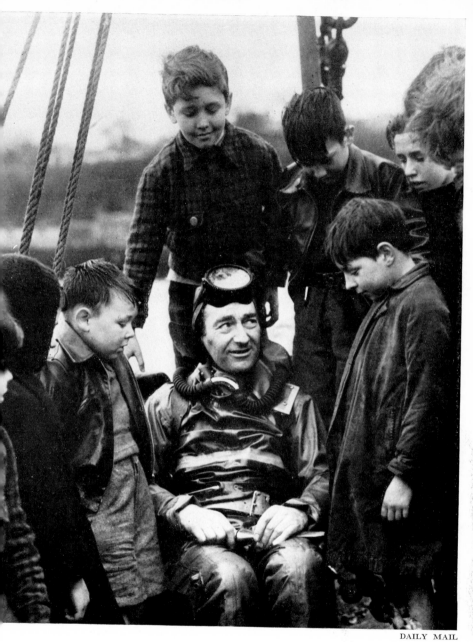

Crabb surrounded by admiring moppets between dives in Tobermory Bay.

As a civilian diver employed by the British Admiralty Research Laboratory at Teddington, Crabb learned to use a 35 millimeter underwater camera.

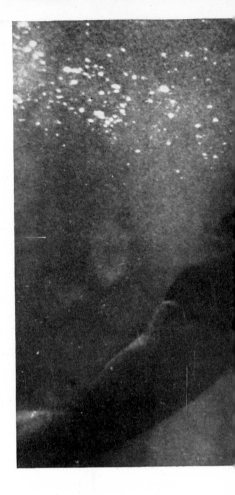

Crabb (right) and British CPO with five captured Italian frogmen who assisted in clearing Venice waters of German mines.

Crabb is a rather appealing and gnome-like figure as he stands shivering while acting as technical advisor for a post war film.

Underwater Working Party. Gibraltar 1942-43.

Seaman A. C. Thomas, the diver who couldn't swim a stroke.

Lt. Crabb at Gibraltar in 1942. Note diving equipment which was obsolete even then.

Underwater shot of Crab[
wearing same type [
equipment he wore on h
last dive.

Sydney James Knowles (center) refreshes himself at the Hotel Mishnish (Gaelic, meaning "The Sanctuary of the Young Deer") in Tobermory during search for the sunken Spanish galleon.

absorbent quality of the granules in the canister had been lost. They changed the canister on each set at least once a fortnight.

Signalman Joseph 'Rattler' Morgan was particularly proud of his job and his equipment and he was hurt one day to find a short, red-haired petty officer examining his gear with obvious distaste. Chief Petty Officer Ralph Thorpe had not heard of the Underwater Working Party. He had come ashore from the destroyer *Brilliant* and he was on his way to the bank when he encountered this collection of junk. Thorpe was feeling miserable. He was a former instructor in Davis Escape Apparatus, considered medically unfit for further sea service and being sent home.

'So this is yours?' he asked Morgan in a deceptively quiet voice. 'Yes, Chief,' said Morgan, holding up his chin. The Chief Petty Officer bent down and rapped an oxygen bottle. A full bottle rings; the bottle which Thorpe rapped gave a very dull sound. 'Were you intending to use this?' 'Yes, Chief. The bottle's been filled.' 'Filled from what?' 'A big flask of oxygen, Chief.' The Chief Petty Officer moaned to the Bay. The only way to keep up a proper pressure in the air bottles was to use an oxygen booster pump. 'What's wrong with your oxygen booster pump?' Morgan said nothing. He was always loyal to his officers. He had never heard of an oxygen booster pump and he was pretty sure that they hadn't. Thorpe was becoming alarmed. He asked if

65

the CO_2 absorbent canister on the set had been changed. 'Yes, Chief, changed it myself, about a week or ten days ago.' The Chief Petty Officer muttered something about the Charge of the Light Brigade. The CO_2 absorbent had to be changed every time the set was used. This Admiralty instruction had been distributed in 1934:

> The CO_2 absorbent granules must be renewed after use when the set is laid aside prior to further practice. Remember that breath on the granules starts the chemical reaction which continues after breathing ceases, so that in a very short time all the granules are useless. So remember that if you do breathe on the granules and leave them you might not be the one to wear that set in a case of emergency . . . you therefore might, perhaps, commit murder.

In the winter of 1942–43 the Underwater Working Party breathed on their granules, put the sets aside and continued to use the same soda lime as CO_2 absorbent for as long as a fortnight. They were the people who used the sets in emergency, and therefore might, perhaps, have been attempting suicide.

Thorpe asked a few more questions, visited the bank, returned to his ship and requested to be transferred to the Underwater Working Party. He acknowledged that he was considered medically unfit for service, but he argued that that only applied to sea service and that the Underwater Working Party was a shore team. Morgan reported to Crabb, who contacted Thorpe that

afternoon. His posting was granted and he joined on
1st January, 1943. He was forty-seven years old and
he had been a naval pensioner when war broke out.
Crabb, aged thirty-two, had begun to dive two years
over the maximum age allowed for trainee divers. He
believed and said, 'A good diver can go on until he's
seventy. There are certain reserves you can call on
when it's necessary, when you have something important to do. The reserves don't come from the body.
They come from some sort of spiritual stimulation.'
In his initial selection of volunteers, Crabb had a wildly
illogical method: he looked for men with bold noses.
Chief Petty Officer Thorpe had a well-developed nose.

He explained booster pumps, the need to renew the
CO_2 absorbent granules, and all the proper drills for
Davis Submerged Escape Apparatus. He also serviced
the sets. After his first dive in a set Thorpe had serviced,
Crabb surfaced leisurely, like a man in a warm bath.
He had not known that breathing under water could
yield such luxury.

A more elaborate system of training began at once.
The Party found a disused ship's boiler 17 feet by 12
which had been used, and discarded, as an air-raid
shelter. Port-holes were cut in the tank and a training
platform built round the open end. The tank was towed
out into Rosia Bay, upended and connected to the water
distillery so that in cold weather it had warmed water
circulating—salt water which had been cooling the

67

distillery plant. For two months the Party spent their days on this preparation and training, and dived at nights.

Training volunteers in the tank, Thorpe tried to make things simple. 'I made things *so* simple with the Davis gear,' he has recalled, 'that I thought I was putting fellows at ease. I had one volunteer from a corvette who was ever so eager. I told him, before he went in, that I was going to make it so simple that he would just go down and think nothing of it. I put my Davis gear on and went in, went down to the bottom of the tank, came up and put my thumbs up to him. He smiled at me. Then I started to go down head first, and of course my feet were up in the air. When I came to the surface I did several somersaults, and when I came out this fellow was crying. I don't know what happened to him. He just said to me, "I can't do that. I mustn't do that. No, no, I don't want to volunteer." He was the only one who ever failed me.'

Petty Officer David Bell replaced Leading Seaman Bell. (They were not related.) The Party then had two officers, two petty officers, two rating divers, and Ordinary Seaman A. C. Thomas as general handyman and sweeper-up. Thomas had been brought up in Wales by two aunts. He was shy, retiring and inclined to blush. His primary naval training had been very swift and he preferred to remove his cap rather than salute when he met an officer. In a naval barracks in England a petty officer had sneered at the manner in which Thomas saluted, and he did not intend to be sneered at again. From his previous hard experience with the Navy, he was always afraid of leg-pulls. When Thorpe sent him to stores for a pair of foot-prints, he had first to be persuaded that foot-prints existed as items of equipment, listed in the Rate Book. He did not mix with the other ratings, he did not drink, he seemed to spend most of his off-duty time in writing home. None of the others learned his Christian name or managed to make friends with him; he was known always as 'Young Thomas'.

Leaning on his sweeping brush, Thomas listened to Thorpe's lectures, entranced. Very quickly, he was better versed in the theory of diving than the divers were. Eventually he went to Thorpe, removed his cap, offered a nervous jerky bow and asked, his voice hoarse with embarrassment, if he could be allowed to learn to dive. He explained that he couldn't swim a stroke, but what with the buoyancy of the DSEA set and all that, perhaps a non-swimmer could be useful now and then. Thorpe was strangely touched, and he spent a month concentrating on Thomas, coaxing him down the ladder of the training tank, step by step. Three weeks passed before Thomas was persuaded to descend to the bottom rung of the ladder, then to make a free ascent in his gear, to be dragged out at the top of the tank. Thereafter, he paraded for extra dips every day. He became completely confident of his equipment. He still could not swim a single stroke on the surface and he evaded all attempts to make him learn, but Crabb was prevailed upon to let him try diving beneath ships in the harbour.

Thomas proved the safest rating diver of the Party, never scared of the water or of being swept away, carrying out his duties according to the letter of the drill that Thorpe had taught him. He searched like an eager mine dog. To get down to the job, he had to leap from the diving-launch to the bottom line of the ship and hold on. When he came up at the stern after his dive, the crew of the launch had to get a heaving-line round him quickly, as he began to float away. Under water with his breathing apparatus and his buoyancy bag he could use his arms and move as well as the next man.

When the others began to stop worrying about Thomas, he vanished one day in 23 feet of water. Crabb gave him the normal time to surface astern and be picked up by the heaving-line. The time passed; three more minutes passed, three more minutes for a man who could not swim.

Crabb dived over the side. On the ship's keel there was no sign of the seaman, but he suddenly saw a pair of heels going up from the rudder. He followed Thomas to the surface, grabbed him to make quite sure there would not be an accident and dragged him inboard.

'Thomas,' he said, angry in his relief, 'where the hell have you been?'

'I was held up,' said Thomas, blushing.

'What held you up?'

'Got caught short,' said Thomas.

Two officers, two petty officers, three rating divers, one of whom could not swim; the Party was still too small.

Stoker Sydney James Knowles had wanted to be a naval diver since he was very young. His father planned to make him a boy bugler in the Army, but Sydney James could not see what opportunity a boy bugler would have for swimming. He had enlisted as a stoker when war broke out, for there seemed no other way of entering the Navy. In the Underwater Working Party he saw his opportunity. His messmates in the destroyer *Lookout,* escorting Malta convoys, assured him that he would be swimming soon enough. Knowles, undeterred, volunteered, and he later explained: 'In the Med. there's a lovely sunny bottom and beautiful green weed and underwater flowers and all that. When you're down there, meeting fish and one thing and another, you get the feeling "I'm king down here, this is all mine." You can't see very far, of course, but you know that this goes on, right along the bottom of the Atlantic and the Pacific and right round the world, and it's all yours, like. . . . It's hard to describe, but that's roughly how I felt about it.'

Knowles, a natural diver, was trained in a matter of hours; today, a clearance diver has a 22-week course. Towards the end of hostilities port-clearance parties used to go home on leave after a major operation; Knowles was to have his next leave at the end of the war, a considerable time after his father had written to Admiral Sir John Cunningham, C-in-C. Mediterranean, to complain that his son had not written for three years and seemed too busy to come home. Sir John, who was also busy, sent a courteous but evasive reply.

The Underwater Working Party had the usual high morale of a special show. The legend of how Bailey and Crabb had dealt with mines and enemy frogmen grew as the Party ratings went slumming among men of lesser outfits. The ratings smiled among themselves when outsiders asked them about 'Buster' Crabb. The rating divers had heard from the diving-launch crew about the first limpet mine, and, watching Crabb, they became convinced that he has incapable of fear. Very privately and proudly they called him 'The Toad'.

The Party declined to live in the shore establishment. Drafts of white-knees were always passing through, asking them silly questions and trying to knock off their gear. At inter-Service level it was agreed that the Underwater Working Party and the shore bomb-disposal party should be allowed to occupy Jumper's Bastion, an underground strong-point of a much earlier garrison. On detachment, the rating divers furnished the Bastion as they thought fit, and Morgan brought along four rock lizards to deal with flies, and a cat which he had persuaded to desert the Army. An old seaman attached for rations to the Party had canaries; the petty officer of the bomb-disposal party had an Alsatian bitch with six pups. All but the parrot were welcome. The parrot had originally belonged to Crabb and accorded well with his appearance. He considered the parrot 'a delightful character'. But its wings were growing; it had a habit of wandering and had twice been recovered from the police station. He felt that it would be happier in the zoo down in Jumper's Bastion. The ratings allowed the parrot to stay. From the beginning it was a nuisance, fluttering round the whitewashed ceiling of the mess which so closely resembled a railway tunnel. At mealtimes the parrot perched on a lamp bracket eight feet up the wall, preparing for intruder missions on the food below. It was very happy in the zoo, soaring out over the battery and the naval dockyard by day, chasing sparrows, and beating up the ratings in their hammocks by night. The ratings had to suffer it. They also had to suffer Army cooking, but, as Knowles pointed out, things were worse at Stalingrad.

Once trained, the men searched ships day and night, examining whole convoys in the darkness after false alarms. The ships' bilge keels were so often covered with sharp limpet shells that Petty Officer Bell was confronted by the ratings with a request for gloves.

'Look at my palms,' said Morgan, 'they're like a navigator's chart gone mad. Must have gloves.'

'Gloves?' Bell asked. 'Where do you reckon you are, in Bond Street? Look at my palms. Nothing wrong with them. Tell you how I got them good and hard. By not wearing gloves. Gloves! You'll be asking for brassiers next.' But they had their gloves. Thomas, for one, carried the gloves at his belt and would gravely consider at a ship's bilge keel whether he should use one glove or two. Gloves were the only refinement of equipment that they ever knew.

While they were at work in daylight, the Party was cheered by idle soldiers on troopships and inspired by the rare, heady sight of a few Englishwomen in uniform, high on passenger decks. Petty Officer Bell always seized such moments to bawl out to the diving-launch coxswain, 'Have the dear little divers got their gloves?'

The climate of Gibraltar has been described in a brochure provided by the Central Office of Information as 'Mild and temperate. The mean minimum and maximum temperatures are *winter* 45 degrees F. to 65 degrees F., *summer* 55 degrees to 85 degrees. Average rainfall is 35 inches. Snow and frost are extremely rare.'

This was little consolation to the Underwater Working Party, standing wet and waiting in the night to go down beneath ships. Some even tried diving in a heavy woollen suit, which they called John Ls. They believed that the water filled up the pores in the wool, trapping warm air inside, and that the warm air would remain there until they had finished their inspections.

Admiral Sir Frederick Edward-Collins, temporary Governor of Gibraltar, was impressed when he saw the men at work. He discovered that their extra pay was locally and quite unofficially fixed at 9d. a day for a rating, 1s. 3d. for a petty officer and 1s. 6d. for an officer. Sir Frederick decreed that this was nonsense and that all ranks should be paid an extra half-crown for every dive. Two sides of a ship would be considered two dives. 'Now what more can I get you?' Sir Frederick asked, and Crabb replied, 'The water is cold, sir. May I suggest an extra issue of rum?'

CHAPTER 5

OPERATION TADPOLE

A WILD WIT at Gibraltar chose Operation Tadpole as the code name for action against the Italian Tenth Flotilla. Crabb's ratings did not use the code. They said 'Flap on in the harbour. Panic stations, Jack'. The Party was too small, too starved of reasonable equipment for grandiose operations.

False alarms rang with ferocious regularity. The harbour defence echo-sounders picked up a block of floating wood. Panic stations, Jack. A sentry saw bubbles in the Bay. Panic stations, Jack. A skipper ordered his ship's bottom to be swept for mines; the sweeping line caught in a crack in the bilge keel; the crack was mistaken for a mine, and the alarm signal, two white lights at the yardarm, was hoisted. Panic stations, Jack.

But on 8th May 1943, when the moon was weak and a storm was rising, Crabb did not like the signs. Operation Tadpole was signalled. The stand-by divers were summoned from their bunks in Jumper's Bastion and he ordered, 'Ten minutes' hell.' On the harbour defence launches, his bomb-disposal ratings lit charges and threw them overboard as fast as they could. The Northover projectors bravely banged away. When ten minutes had passed, charge-dropping was stopped in one area, while the Underwater Working Party went over the side.

Crabb had six divers, with more than sixty ships in the Roads and no certainty that there had been an attack. They had to choose where to start, where to search in the storm and the dark, where to work a way along a bilge keel and try to establish by touch the presence of a torpedo warhead or a mine.

As usual, there were few bottom lines rigged. When divers climbed on board merchantmen and talked about Italian frogmen, they were regarded as Rock-happy by the crews. Crabb sometimes thought that the Italians might have more success if they simply chose the more sleepy ships, climbed on board and placed their charges inboard. On one ship there was not even a watch-keeper and he walked, unchallenged, to the master's cabin.

Twenty-five ships of a convoy which was sailing at 7 A.M. had first to be searched and cleared. For speed they worked two men to a ship, one at either side. On twelve of the ships they had to clamber aboard and explain their needs to officers who grumbled about turning men out in the night. Then the divers had to stand wet, waiting, numb with cold. Chief Petty Officer Thorpe, quite unfit for active service, went diving with the others, to ease the strain.

The first convoy was clear of warheads, but another was not. Normally Crabb selected by hunch the ships to be searched, as a man will choose a horse; but that night his luck was out. At dawn, a charge exploded beneath the United States Liberty ship *Pat Harrison,* and explosions under the British ships *Mahsud* and *Camerata* followed. Lifeboats began drifting. Thorpe's clearest memory of the dawn is of an Indian crew lining the deck, each man with his boots tied round his neck, preparing to abandon ship. In a launch, Commander Hancock raced alongside, shouting to ships' officers to get their vessels into shallow water before they went down. The three ships were towed but the work was not done. On the bilge keel of the *Pat Harrison* Crabb found a mine that the Italians had placed for good measure. It had not exploded, for the warhead's explosion had stopped the mine's clocks.

In the morning, Spanish patrols on the north coast of the Bay found diving equipment, placed in studied disarray by Italian agents, to convince the British that the marauders had come from a parent submarine, scuttled their torpedoes and gone ashore in the north.

Bailey and Crabb were not impressed. They suspected that this attack had come from Algeciras. Intelligence officers did not discount the possibility that the *Olterra* had some connection with the raids, but there were no signs of unusual activity on board. Only a diver could have discovered the torpedo door beneath the water-line.

Crabb and Bailey volunteered to do a little intelligence work of their own, by swimming round the *Olterra* after dark. They were forbidden to do anything of the kind. The Navy would not countenance the search of a ship in a neutral port. The higher the diving officers appealed the more firm was the refusal. They remained suspicious of the *Olterra*, but they had little time for speculation. A disastrous summer was beginning.

A Liberator carrying General Sikorsky to England from the Middle East crashed into the water just beyond the runway of Gibraltar, and the great Sikorsky died with his daughter and sixteen others.

The Polish military leader was found floating, but there were bodies trapped in the plane. Sikorsky's papers had to be recovered, in case they were washed ashore in Spain. Bailey and Crabb dived on the following day. As they reached the plane, they saw something caught on a wing, swaying with the current: a headless man. They surfaced and announced that they were dissatisfied with their breathing-gear.

79

When they dived again, they discovered that the object on the wing was an overcoat. In the plane they found the general's brief-case. Beyond lay broken bags of microfilm mail, intended for home by soldiers of the Middle East. Broken cigarette cartons were tingeing the water green. Bodies had to be removed, every scrap of paper in the aeroplane had to be retrieved.

While the officers dived to the plane on six successive days, Petty Officer Bell examined ships from Spanish ports collecting at Gibraltar to join convoys. On the sixth day he found a limpet mine and reported his find to an officer who was not a diver. The officer ordered him to remove it, although he was well aware that petty officers were not allowed to touch enemy mines. When Bell had taken the mine from the ship and had moored it beneath a buoy, a naval intelligence officer took over. He rowed the mine towards the rock in Rosia Bay, until a lop rose on the water and the rowing-boat seemed in danger of sinking. The officer did not fancy swimming ashore, towing a mine which might explode. He threw off the rope to the buoy, expecting the buoy to mark the mine.

The buoy vanished beneath the waves, dragged down by the mine. The intelligence officer was horrified. The dinghy suddenly seemed quite safe; the lop had as suddenly subsided. He took careful cross-bearings before he rowed to the shore. Crabb was called from the Liberator to find the missing mine. He was tired, and he explained a little testily that he was not clairvoyant. Had Petty Officer Bell been allowed to finish examining the ship, after he found the mine? He had not. Crabb dived to the ship in the evening and found another mine, on the other side. This mine was of an entirely new design, the first specimen of an excellent Italian model which was to be used a great deal. In such a mine the possibility of a booby-trap could not be discounted. Crabb discovered that there was no booby-trap by the usual process of finding out by experiment.

The following morning Admiral Sir Frederick Edward-Collins ordered that the missing mine under the buoy must be recovered. Crabb rubbed his hand in his beard; 'On the face of it,' he said, 'the order is a trifle presumptuous.'

A night had passed, the mine would soon explode, and it lay in deep water. Rosia Bay was used by swimmers for pleasure, and the Admiral was particularly anxious that pleasure swimmers should not be blown up. Crabb set out with Bell, two motor-boats, a light line and little hope. He intended to sweep the bottom with the line, and he felt as if he were setting out with a minnow net to fish for basking shark. His face was long, and in the other boat the face of Petty Officer Bell was longer. In the area indicated by the cross-bearings Crabb hesitated, then decided to have a trial swim before he began sweeping.

Diving to thirty feet he saw what he took to be a

jelly-fish beneath him. The 'jelly-fish' proved to be the buoy floating above the mine. All that remained was to get a rope round the buoy and heave it to the surface. In the excitement of finding the mine, they forgot that it might explode. It seemed an extraordinary piece of luck, and good luck was appreciated in the summer of 1943.

Lieutenant Bailey was not too well. He was regularly sick after dives. Afraid that his lungs might be affected, Crabb persuaded him to ease off on routine diving, and himself inevitably became the only diving officer on watch. He gave up trying to spend his nights ashore. At nine each night, he boarded a harbour defence launch with a bomb-disposal rating and the duty diver, to sleep in the small wardroom of the launch until the first alarm of the night, when he turned out until the job was done.

At seven each morning he left the launch and went back to his flat for a bath and breakfast, before the routine day began. Then he made out the signals for patrols and charge-dropping, he checked on depth-charges being made up for the night to come, he visited the Northover projectors. The Sea Transport Officer also required divers to inspect the propellers of merchant ships in the bay. The tank in Rosia Bay, the Underwater Working Party's training place, became as well the official practice tank for submarine crews enduring their periodic refreshers in the use of Davis escape gear. On Wednesday mornings, inter-Service bomb-disposal meetings were held.

For variety, Italian saboteurs in neutral ports began to drop their explosives inboard. From the Germans they had acquired pieces of 'coal' which would set a ship's bunkers alight, fibre cases which would burst into flame, fruit which contained the seeds of destruction. Normally, all ships from neutral ports were examined in Rosia Bay when they arrived. Once, during the pressure of work, a ship came unchecked into the coaling wharf. Crabb dived in haste, found nothing underneath and declared her clear. Just before lunch the ship moved out to moorings and there was a loud explosion. The hold was found to be a mass of pulped oranges. It took ten days to trace the evidence of a bomb, not on the keel, but in a hold among the orange-crates.

False alarms began day by day. One morning the launch raced out to a War Department vessel loaded with ammunition and explosives which was about to be abandoned by her crew. As the master put it, they could hear a 'ticking'. There was indeed a ticking, a ticking which sounded like the grandfather of all clocks, a most unnerving sound aboard a ship with the fire risk of a Catherine wheel. The engineer was ordered to stop all auxiliary engines, and the tick was menacingly louder. The crew were taken off in the launch while Crabb and Thorpe searched the engine-room, searched the hold, had deck-plates pulled up in the engine-room. Crabb dived to examine the bottom of the ship, and in the water the ticking was soft but still insistent.

He surfaced, took off his mask and suddenly saw the source of the trouble. Two cable-lengths away, a salvage vessel was at work with her large pumps. The ticking noise came from the pumps; the noise was carried through the water to the explosives ship on an odd current. The launch was called back alongside and the crew were persuaded back on board. The anchor was raised and the ship steamed clear of the salvage ship; when she was stopped, the ticking had gone.

When Bailey was posted home, later to distinguish himself in the port party which cleared Caen harbour of mines under shell-fire, a relieving officer was sent out from England. Despite his excellent intentions, he had asthma and could not dive. He was relieved by Lieutenant Hood, a brave man who detested diving but still was determined to do the job. Hood disappeared under a keel on his first operational clearance.

He dived in clear water on a sunny day, under the port side of a merchant vessel, while a rating diver went down to starboard. Five minutes later the rating surfaced and signalled that his side was clear. Two more minutes passed. It would not do to chase an officer on his first operational dive. Another minute passed, with the seconds limping. Then Crabb dived, searched the ship's bottom, surfaced to order the other divers over the side and went down again.

As each diver surfaced, he held up a hand with the thumb turned down. One by one they came in from the search, boarding the launch listlessly. They had nothing to say. The body was not recovered for a fortnight. Hood's goggles and his breathing gear had been dragged down round his neck in his last struggles for breath.

It was a summer of death and destruction. One morning when most of the team were servicing sets in their operational hut on the North Mole, not far from the edge of the runway, they heard a plane coming in very low. Crabb got out of the hut in time to see an Albacore crash into the Water Port in twenty feet of water. He ran down with his diving gear, kicking off his shoes, the team straggling out behind him. They struck out, with the strange and burning sensation of swimming in pure petrol, to the plane with its broken wing, but they were at least five minutes too late to save any of the crew.

When they landed, Chief Petty Officer Thorpe was on the quay waiting. 'Sir,' said the Chief, 'they've sunk our boat.' Unnoticed in the emergency, a cable-layer had casually entered the pen where the diving-launch lay. She had too much way on her, and before either her engines or her backsprings could pull her up she had crushed the launch amidships. Knowles, still officially a stoker, had been examining the engine of the diving-launch to see if he could learn about her and blind his mates with science; he got on deck just in time.

The launch was on the bottom, 'broken', as Thorpe said, 'like a biscuit in the hand'. For the next three weeks the Underwater Working Party did not have a boat that they could call their own, for the Navy was short of harbour craft. Crabb engaged himself in humiliating negotiations, eventually wheedling the loan of a bomb scow from the Royal Air Force.

CHAPTER 6

THE HOUR
OF
TRIAL

SPANISH bumboats came alongside the troopships lying at Gibraltar to sell their loads of fruit and watches, cigarettes and chocolate. It occurred to Crabb that it would be simple enough for a swimmer to hang on the bottom of a bumboat and fix a limpet mine to a troopship, while the bumboat continued its shrill business.

The thought had also occurred to a regular member of one bumboat's crew. In dirty beret and greasy sweater, Dr. Elvio Moscatelli of the Italian Tenth Light Flotilla often put out from Algeciras in a bumboat. Dr. Moscatelli was captain of the *Olterra*. He was also surgeon and intelligence officer of the Tenth in their underwater attacks on Gibraltar. The piloted torpedo crews had been re-formed. From the *Olterra* a 24-hour watch

87

was being kept on the ships entering Gibraltar, and Moscatelli's excursions to Gibraltar by bumboat ensured a good close look at the job. He knew Crabb and the Underwater Party well by sight and particularly liked to watch them searching ships for mines and warheads which were not there. This work would tire them out before the major attacks to come. He learned too to recognise the bomb scow as he had the diving-launch.

In Gibraltar, fresh water was in very short supply. A Spanish waterboat regularly sailed to Algeciras and returned, to pipe off its supplies in the harbour. Moscatelli intended to have a piloted torpedo hanging on below the waterboat like a sucker fish beneath a shark. The torpedo crew could place a warhead on a capital ship, shielded by a Spanish waterboat from the mighty British Navy.

But Crabb anticipated this dea. He sent a diver down to examine the waterboat each time it reached Gibraltar. Knowles and Morgan checked it regularly and were on excellent terms with the crew.

Morgan, as the rating diver with the longest experience, had made three trips to Spain, signing on British merchantmen as an able seaman. His orders were to wait until his ship was ready to leave the Spanish port on its return trip to Gibraltar, then dive round its side to check whether it had been mined while it lay at anchor. In the process, Morgan acquired a taste for counter-espionage.

He, Frazer and Knowles had discarded a private
theory that the enemy was dropped by parachute. In
Jumper's Bastion Morgan strongly upheld a view which
Crabb had unintentionally passed on to him. He maintained that the enemy came from the *Olterra*. It stood
to reason, Morgan argued, that the Italian tanker wasn't
lying there for nothing. He hinted that he had heard
something from the crew of the waterboat, something
which backed his suspicion.

Stoker Knowles has recalled part of a conversation:

' "Wouldn't it be funny," one of us said, "if we met
up with the Italians when this lot's over? We'd have a
rare old party together, to old times and all that." We
wondered what type of characters these Italians were
like, and I think it was Rattler Morgan who said that
they must be much the same as we were, with a Morgan
and a Frazer and a Thomas type among them. We felt
more close to the swimmers than the chaps who rode
the pigs, because the swimmers, like us, were riding on
nothing. Thomas said nothing. He never did. He was
always writing home.'

Crabb had become a Lieutenant-Commander and
had been awarded the George Medal. But he was
obviously overworked and they wanted to help him.
Morgan and Knowles decided to find out about the
Olterra on their day off. They arranged to make the
passage in the Algeciras waterboat, after protracted and
secret negotiations with the crew. For the journey they

dressed as Spanish seamen, as elaborately disguised as any member of the *Olterra*'s crew. Against all orders, they slipped back aboard the waterboat one afternoon and sailed to Algeciras.

'We had,' Knowles said, 'to watch the Spanish guards, but we got tipped off by the waterboat crew when to slip ashore. We walked along the jetty and there was the *Olterra* sitting there, quite plain. Morgan suspected even more strongly that Lieutenant-Commander Crabb was right. In fact, he didn't suspect it, he ruddy well knew, and there was me not believing him.'

They hesitated at the *Olterra*. There was a Spanish sentry on the gangway and they didn't want to risk their Spanish on him. Lounging on deck were Italian seamen of the Tenth Flotilla, still dramatically disguised, still shuffling and spitting and wiping noses on their sleeves, as they had been taught in their special merchant seamen course at Leghorn.

Knowles and Morgan reconnoitered the *Olterra* stylishly, as they had learned in the cinema at home. There seemed no way of getting on board, or, once on board, of remaining undetected. There was nothing which suggested swimmers or two-man-torpedo operators. Reluctantly the counter-espionage file of the Underwater Working Party left the *Olterra*'s side and went into a café to consider their next move.

The café that they chose was patronised by the Italians from the *Olterra*. Italian naval ratings, disguised as loafers, gazed at British naval ratings disguised as loafers, and the British naval ratings gazed back. The café was regularly visited by British agents, Italian agents, German agents and Spanish agents. The afternoon was heady with conspiracy. Knowles wanted to get a seat by the window so that he could watch the *Olterra*. He tried to persuade the café proprietor to give him a window seat, but he was not equal to the task of whispering in Spanish.

In the end they left the café; they had to get back to the waterboat, for she had to be back at Gibraltar before dusk. Back in Gibraltar, they stayed out of sight while other divers examined her. They played cards with Spanish seamen below decks until ten minutes to nine, ten minutes before the curfew. At the end of the last game, the card school scattered, the Spanish seamen making for the border and La Linea; Knowles and Morgan making for their uniforms hidden in a shed. As they headed for the shed, a military policeman bore down on them on a motor-cycle.

'You know what we'll get for this,' said Morgan. 'Ninety days. *Ninety* days, but we might pull a fast one on him when all's said and done.'

The British military policeman stopped.

'Nueve o'clock,' he said menacingly.

'No comprender,' Knowles replied.

'Nueve o'clock,' said the policeman, pointing towards the frontier.

91

'Labor noche,' Knowles said. Night work, he meant. They were allowed to walk away.

'A right near do, was that,' said Knowles.

From its bracket the Jumper's Bastion parrot mocked them as they climbed into their bunks. Thomas was still writing home. Crabb was settling in aboard the defence launch for another night of waiting and slumbering, before another false alarm and yet another dip in the moonlight. As he fell asleep, the defense launch began its run, round the ships at anchor in the Roads.

The modified Northover projectors were still firing at every alarm, and were slowly blasting cracks in the harbour walls. But the Underwater Working Party had a new secret weapon. This was a barbed-wire curtain and it was very easily rigged round a ship. A light wire ran fore and aft along the ship, about six feet above the bilge keel. From this wire, at ten-foot intervals, fifteen-foot lengths of barbed wire depended, every second length being weighted. In the dark the Italians would run straight into the wire and tear their rubber suits before they could place a warhead or a mine. The wires were so well concealed that Knowles had run into such a curtain in daylight and ripped his buoyancy bag.

Although the curtain was very simple to rig, few merchant captains would be persuaded to try it. Crabb could not provide an underwater rigging party for every ship at anchor in Gibraltar. Here and there, at very wide intervals, a captain appreciated the plan and rigged such a curtain for himself. The captain of the British steamer *Stanridge* was one such.

On the night of 3rd August 1943, the deep door of the *Olterra* closed behind three piloted torpedoes. Commander Ernesto Notari led the attack. He was approaching forty, and was a far more cautious, if no less skilful, charioteer than Visintini. He had decided that the harbour could not be entered lightly and should be ignored. Having been a salvage expert, he had chosen his targets with discrimination. His diver, Giannolli, was a new man with very little experience of two-man-torpedo work.

Notari took his torpedo in a wide sweep north round the Bay to keep out of the main path of the searchlights, diving when a defence launch seemed too close, surfacing again when the launch passed by, heading for the *Stanridge*. He came close enough to hear men talking and to see the glow of cigarettes, to know that he was attacking men and not just a float of steel. Then he warned Giannolli behind him and dived for the *Stanridge*'s bilge keel.

He dived into the deeper dark, and suddenly something was tearing at his mask, rocking the chariot, tearing holes in his rubber suit. A lesser man might have given up, but he dived deeper and beneath the barbed wire. Notari had a printed order to cover such contingencies, which read:

Your life is precious, but the objective is more precious. This must be remembered in the moment of action. Repeat it to yourself a hundred times a day, and swear you will not fail in the hour of trial.

They were ready now to apply the drill. Diver Giannolli left his seat and swam for the ship. He fixed a clamp on the port side of the bilge keel of the *Stanridge* and a clamp on the starboard side. The time-fuse of the warhead was set. It was about to be disconnected and hung between the two clamps on a length of rope. Giannolli was understandably nervous, and he was cold as water seeped into his torn suit. His hands faltered and he dropped the rope. So he had to clamp the warhead directly to the port side of the bilge keel.

In the delay, their torpedo suddenly lost her trim and her nose went up as if she intended to surface . . . alongside the *Stanridge,* in full view of any man who happened to be on deck. Notari fought to correct his trim, to keep the nose down, and the torpedo dived for the bottom of the Bay, out of control, taking Notari with her while his diver still hung to the bilge keel of the *Stanridge.*

The torpedo plunged to 112 feet, its maximum diving depth, and went diving on. Somehow Notari kept his wits. He managed to blow his main ballast tank and began to pump the water from his trimming tanks. The nose went up, the torpedo rushed for the surface. As the water pressure decreased, Notari's breathing-bag expanded and his face-piece was blown off. It seemed unlikely that he would have any further need of it; the torpedo appeared to be taking him up beneath the *Stanridge*, to break his neck. And yet he surfaced with a splash a yard from the ship's side, clear of the barbed wire. He lay over his controls, breathing the good air, waiting for the lights and the shots that would end the night. There were no shots, there were no lights. He recovered and remembered his diver.

'Giannolli, Giannolli,' he whispered.

When he could wait no longer by the ship's side, Notari tried to make for home. He could not dive with his erratic machine and his torn suit, without his breathing gear. His pig would cruise only at full speed ahead. He had four miles to travel on the surface with a fiery wake to betray him to patrol boats. On such a night, with such little contact with normality, Notari should not have been surprised by the intrusion of nonsense. A porpoise was close behind him, treading on his tail. A school of porpoises came playing round, hiding him, destroying his wake, conducting him to safety right across the Bay. He thought of it, later, as a miracle.

At Gibraltar, the alarm had not been given. In his launch on his normal patrol, Crabb caught the silhouette of the Norwegian tanker *Thoshovdi*. He remembered

95

bitterly that he had protested that the tanker was anchored too close to Algeciras. He still suspected Algeciras, and his suspicions were still ignored. The crew of another piloted torpedo had fixed the warhead which would blow the tanker *Thoshovdi* in two. The crew of the third two-man torpedo had hung their warhead, on its length of line, beneath the 7000-ton American Liberty ship *Harris Gray Otis*. When their work was completed, the chariots turned away and arrived safely back in Algeciras.

Diver Giannolli alone remained. When his torpedo plunged he had swum from the bilge keel to the surface. He was swimming there when Notari surfaced on the far side of the ship. Giannolli decided that the torpedo was on the bottom and that Notari had drowned. He would not give himself up before the other torpedo crews had had time to make their escape. He remembered the drill. He swam astern of the *Stanridge*, carefully avoiding the wire, and sat on the rudder while he stripped off his diving gear and sank it. Then he sat there, shivering in his underwear, for almost two hours. This was long enough. He dropped off the rudder, swam round the side of the *Stanridge* and shouted for help.

He was dragged on board. The captain of the *Stanridge* immediately signalled the shore. Crabb was signalled, and his launch turned towards the *Stanridge* from the far end of the Roads. Petty Officer Bell raced for the *Stanridge* with the second launch and reached her first. Bell took Giannolli on board his launch, where he was questioned, while the boat bobbed up and down by the port side of the *Stanridge*, above the warhead which was due to explode. Sitting in the wheelhouse, Giannolli had nothing to say.

The obvious place to begin searching was on the port side where they were. Bell stripped off his clothes and fixed his breathing apparatus. He got on the jumping ladder to go. He had one foot in the water when the warhead went up, and the launch was covered in splinters and spume. One splinter went through the wheelhouse and killed the sentry standing over the silent Giannolli. Giannolli was unmarked. A second splinter struck Bell, as he was poised with one foot in the water. Having missed death by a second, he got a black eye.

As Crabb's launch raced on towards the listing *Stanridge*, the Norwegian tanker broke in two and the *Harrison Gray Otis* exploded. The Underwater Working Party were diving for the rest of the night in search of more warheads, while the heavy oil from the Norwegian tanker drifted across the Bay. Petty Officer Bell was searching bilge keels with the others within an hour. He had been badly shaken, and his eye was closing. He then worked through the night. For earlier work with the Underwater Working Party, Petty Officer Bell had been awarded the George Medal. The others felt that he had earned it again.

97

Chief Petty Officer Thorpe had been in hospital through all the excitement, to his ill-concealed disgust. He was having trouble with his stomach and with his ears; his face was badly blistered and swollen with his continual diving in the Bay and in the training tank, day after day, beyond his strength.

When he returned to duty, he remarked coldly on the condition of the ratings' lanyards. He stalked the holes in their socks. He insisted that they applied the proper Davis Escape Apparatus drill—including floating on their backs when they surfaced after clearing a ship.

'You're a scruffy-looking lot,' said the Chief. 'Sunday morning we'll have divisions for the four of you.'

'Divisions, Chief?' asked Stoker Knowles. 'Will we fall in, four deep?'

With Crabb the Chief was equally strict. On a routine daylight examination of ships, a troop-carrying liner in the Bay was reported attacked and the swimmer alarm was given. As the divers' launch came alongside Crabb quickly got out of his clothes. The ship was in deep water and it might go down very soon. He fitted a breathing set and dived. There were no mines on the bottom of the ship; it had been a false alarm. When he regained the launch he found C.P.O. Thorpe was in genuine alarm.

'Put that gear away quickly, sir,' he said, 'and get below.'

Out of the ratings' hearing, he continued: 'Sir, I

wish you wouldn't do that sort of thing. Sir, there were ATS aboard that ship. You must collect your bathing-trunks and put them on before you go into the water.'

'Chief, this was an emergency, and I had to get into the water as quickly as I could.'

'Sir, this is a question of discipline. I don't care how urgent it was. You mustn't just jump into the water in front of these young women or your ratings. Please don't do it again.'

Thorpe began also, in Crabb's words, 'to ride Petty Officer Bell to hell', and Crabb watched apprehensively. He knew as well as Thorpe how necessary it was to tighten up discipline fast, after a strain like the August attack, but he wondered if Thorpe was not tightening up too fast. He said, 'Chief, don't you think you're a little too hard on Petty Officer Bell? Couldn't you ease up?'

'Sir,' said the Chief, 'he's a very good diver, and I can't take the risk of him getting swollen-headed. That happens to many men when they get medals, even stable characters like Bell. So, when he gets in at nights, I make him scrub his cabin out.'

* * * * *

While the Italian Navy steadily retreated, their Tenth Flotilla advanced. After the August attack another was planned with a new machine, the San Bartolemo piloted torpedo, which could cross all the way from the *Olterra* to Gibraltar submerged. At midday on 2nd October 1943, a diversion was to be created while three San Bartolemo torpedoes slipped into Gibraltar harbour to deal with capital ships.

But in his Tenth Flotilla headquarters at La Spezia on 8th September, Commander Borghese turned on his radio to hear the news, and listened in shocked silence. The announcer had informed him that Italy had been obliged to ask an armistice. Borghese's private war had become so very private that the Italian Navy had not troubled to tell him that the other war was over. In August the Minister of Marine had described the Tenth Flotilla as the spearhead of the Italian Navy. By September the shaft had been broken and the spearhead discarded in a disorderly retreat, as spearheads always are. Or so it appeared to Borghese. He reorganized a land division to fight on the Republican side, and many of his men joined him, impressed by the argument that an honourable man does not change sides in the middle of a war. Others of the Tenth Flotilla considered that the Germans had to be run out of Italy and that the Republicans were Fascists, traitors, or the dupes of Mussolini. They made their way south to join the Allies.

Between attacks, the *Olterra*'s assault crews had been trained in Italy, while the tanker had only a skeleton crew. When the armistice was announced, this crew left forthwith, and a certain Commander Pierleoni found himself almost alone in an attempt to destroy the *Olterra's* gear before it fell into British hands. For Pierleoni, who had arranged for much of the gear to be smuggled in, it was a particularly disagreeable task, but he set the self-destruction charge on one of the piloted torpedoes, ditched the bilge-keel mines, scuttled a quantity of diving equipment then left Spain hurriedly, using his smuggling connections for the last time.

On a morning in September 1943 Crabb learned, quite by chance, that the *Olterra* was being towed into Gibraltar with a Defence Security guard on board. He examined her, and salvaged a piloted torpedo from the floating debris in the forepeak. He reminded no one of how Bailey and he had pleaded to be allowed to swim round the *Olterra*. He had uncharitable thoughts about intelligence and security officers in general but the individual ones he knew struck him as delightful chaps, and one didn't kick people when they were down. When the torpedo was reconstructed, he called her Emily, learned to pilot her, and even shaved off his beard to wear Italian breathing-gear. When Emily dived for the last time, and died of a battery explosion, he thought it was the end of his affair with the Tenth Flotilla.

CHAPTER 7

SIGNAL
FROM LULU

IN THE summer of 1944, Lieutenant-Commander Crabb and Stoker Knowles drove in a truck, over shell-scarred roads, towards Florence. After some dull months in Gibraltar, they had had a bewildering change of fortune. Crabb had been ordered to select one rating diver from the Underwater Working Party and prooceed to Italy. They had entered Leghorn with the Fifth American Army as the clearance diving team of a British naval port party. The port party was charged with rebuilding a supply port from the rubble of Leghorn.

Now, with a truck and a White Ensign flying on the roof of the cab, they were on their way to Florence. Somewhere ahead of them was a rugged outfit known as the Joint Services Intelligence Collecting Unit, com-

posed of Americans and British of all three fighting
Services. When Florence was entered, the unit would
seize important enemy weapons, equipment and documents. Individual officers would search for information
in their own fields. Crabb had been sent from Leghorn
to join them, as an authority on the Italian Tenth Light
Flotilla. In Florence, mines were made.

Knowles was delighted. He had taken to wearing
two .38 revolvers slung low. No one at home would ever
believe that he was involved in counter-espionage, but
he enjoyed the experience for its own sake. Here at last,
he thought was his opportunity to carry a dagger and
to wear a false nose.

Crabb was concentrating upon the road. The naval
contingent of the Intelligence Collecting Unit had last
been reported to the south of Arezzo, which lies to the
south-east of Florence. It was a very fluid war, and
villages were changing hands with extraordinary rapid-
ity. He had no desire to get ahead of the Army. They
reached Arezzo just before dusk and began to make enquiries, but none of the Allied soldiery in the place
knew where I.C.U. was. The officers of an armoured
brigade which was halted by the roadside plainly
doubted that any such unit existed, and Crabb decided
to push on in the general direction of Florence. When
the armoured brigade began to roll along the road and
he found that they were leading it towards action, he
pulled out and withdrew. No instructions in the Manual

of Seamanship covered any such emergency. They drove back, most cautiously, to Arezzo, and Knowles said that his old dad had always wanted him to be a boy bugler in the Army. His companion was silent. He was thinking. A naval diver, about to involve himself in Intelligence in an inland town, could expect the unexpected.

They spent the night in Arezzo and reached the naval contingent of I.C.U. on the following day, encamped in an olive-grove near Poggibonsi, to the south-west of Florence. Florence was to have been an open city, but the Germans, apparently were resisting fiercely. Meantime the naval campers of Poggibonsi paddled in the stream at the bottom of a hill, tried to drop stones on water-beetles, and learned the Italian for 'I love you' and 'Would you care for a tin of bully beef?'

When they eventually moved forward, forded the Arno and entered Florence, a brisk battle between the Germans and the Partisans was still on. The mines which Crabb wanted were in the northern industrial part of the city, still held by the Germans. Knowles was sniped at, and returned fire with his .38s. Their hotel, the Excelsior, was shelled by night, and by day street battles confined them to a few blocks. A Florentine, discovering that Crabb and Knowles were naval divers, assumed that they had come to recover statues which had been blown into the Arno, and implored the divers to be careful with them. Crabb promised himself that if he emerged from this lunacy with a normal mind, he would never think another nasty thought about Intelligence officers.

When he made a most important discovery in Florence, he was at first tempted to suspect that it was part of the magnificent nightmare which was raging around him. A young Italian came to the Allies with information, was passed on to I.C.U., and passed on again to Crabb and Lieutenant Tony Marsloe of the United States Naval Reserve, who worked as a team: Marsloe had Intelligence training and spoke Italian, while Crabb had a knowledge of the enemy.

Together they interrogated the young Italian in the lounge of the Excelsior. He was a dark and slender man of about twenty, dressed in shirt and shorts and wearing the flashes of a Partisan brigade. He introduced himself as Sub-Lieutenant Venturini, recently of the Republican Forces and of the Italian Tenth Flotilla. After a pause, he said that he had changed his mind and had decided to fight for the Partisans. Realising that he was not making headway with the Allied officers, he took out an envelope and a stub of pencil and sketched a new delayed-action limpet mine. It was, he explained, a solid block of explosive cast with a recess in the nose to take the firing mechanism. Centrally round the mine ran a steel band holding a single limpet clamp. Under the clamp was a second recess which held a second detonator and a spring-loaded striker. A saboteur would attach the mine below the bilge-keel ledge of a ship. He would then draw out a safety pin, freeing the spring-loaded striker. After that, any movement of the mine would cause the striker to move and the mine to fire. For example, if an Allied clearance diver tried to slacken the clamp, the striker would move and the mine would explode. Once the safety pin was out, it could not be replaced. The mine was simple and ingenious, like all the better tools of war.

With such mines, Venturini said, the Tenth Flotilla intended to attack ships at anchor in the invaded ports of northwest Italy. Before the Allied Navies had time to build up adequate harbour defences, frogmen saboteurs would be calling. They were a mixed group of assault craft operators and swimmers, based on La Spezia.

It was impossible to signal all Venturini's information, so Crabb packed him into a truck with Knowles and took him south to British Naval Headquarters at Caserta for a full interrogation. Here he was able to give very full details, including the names and the strength of the enemy.

German submarines were being driven from the western Mediterranean, and German surface units were fully engaged in protecting coastal convoys. The Tenth Flotilla alone could provide offensive naval action, but until now the Allies had had no clear proof that the Tenth Flotilla was still operating an underwater unit, for after the armistice Borghese had formed a land division of his own men and the others who had rallied round his flag in La Spezia.

Venturini's news was news indeed, and on the strength of it Naval Headquarters decided to break Crabb's ties with I.C.U. forthwith. He was immediately placed in command of all anti-sabotage diving operations in the North of Italy, with overall command of bomb-safety parties on both coasts so that he could co-ordinate defence. Venturini was to remain with him and serve in whatever capacity Crabb thought fit.

Crabb's specialist knowledge of the Tenth Flotilla was becoming positively embarrassing. Because of it, he had had three changes of job within a matter of weeks. He now had the whole of Northern Italy in which to wage his private war. He remembered the signal from Lulu and had to smile. Lulu was the name by which the Director of Bomb Disposal was known to all his officers. Lulu had trained him at the Cumberland School of Bomb Disposal, named, with Lulu's devastating humour, H.M.S. Volcano. Recently, Lulu had made a secret signal to the Commander-in-Chief Mediterranean, stating that Lieutenant-Commander L. P. K. Crabb, R.N.V.R., G.M., had not undergone a refresher course in England since 1942 and could therefore no longer be considered a competent bomb-safety officer. Competent or otherwise, Crabb now had a fairly large job on his hands.

He set off for Leghorn, only thirty miles south of the

107

enemy base at La Spezia and their most tempting target.

When they reached Leghorn, Crabb reported to the captain in command of the port party and began to prepare. He and Knowles had an intimate knowledge of the harbour, acquired in unusual circumstances. When the port was first entered by the Allies they had searched for mines under the quays, while the quays were being shelled by the Germans. It had been a large task to attempt to clear the harbour of German ground mines, and now it seemed a larger one to defend it against Italian frogmen. The British Navy, concerned in rebuilding the harbour, had had little time to reconstruct the defences.

Although Crabb was now in command of all antisabotage diving in Northern Italy, he could not call upon more clearance divers to help, for the Navy was extremely short of shallow-water divers. Locally, the clearance-diving team would have to consist of himself, Knowles and Venturini. The harbourmaster, an English naval officer, offered him a fourth man. He said that one of his Italian boatmen, who had been cleared by security officers, was a trained diver. It seemed extremely unlikely, but Crabb called at the harbour office to check up. The boatman was a very strongly built Italian peasant who gave his name as Vago Giari. Giari admitted straight away that he had been involved in the swimming attacks upon Gibraltar before Crabb arrived there. For this he had been awarded the Italian Gold

Medal. It was he who had badly damaged the steamer *Raven's Point,* and it was he, he was ashamed to say, who had pushed a comrade's head under water when an argument developed on who should place his mine upon that ship. After the armistice he had retired quietly to his cottage on the outskirts of Leghorn. He had volunteered to do a little boating for the British to make some money. Now he would like to return to diving. Giari considered that the war had gone on too long.

Entered in the books as 'Italian labour', Giari served in the Underwater Working Party, Leghorn, as an Italian version of Chief Petty Officer Thorpe. He was much the strongest swimmer of the party, and he taught the others the correct way to use Italian swimfins and diving-suits. They had still to capture Italian breathing-gear and they used DSEA sets, to Giari's disgust. He did not care to swim with a submariner's escape outfit, and he was always complaining to Knowles that he had been far better off at Gibraltar. Days and weeks passed without an attack, while Giari and Knowles became firm friends. While the Italian explained the finer points of his excursions to Gibraltar, Knowles dwelt on the technique of clearance diving. In their conversations a note of rivalry occasionally intruded. Giari would mention, off-handedly, that a chap he knew had placed a most beautiful bomb on a steamer at Huelva, and Knowles said that a chap he knew had taken it off.

109

While barbed-wire defences were built, while destroyers prepared light depth-charges to Crabb's specifications, while patrols were increased and naval intelligence and security officers built up a picture of the enemy, a certain Commander Ernesto Notari of the Italian Navy called at Navy House in Leghorn, announced himself as an old colleague of Petty Officer Giari of the Underwater Working Party and asked to see Lieutenant-Commander Crabb. Crabb entered the room, and was most surprised when the Italian walked forward affably and shook his hand. He thanked Crabb for his gesture in burying Visintini at sea off Gibraltar, in 1942. He explained that he had taken command of the attacks from the *Olterra* after Visintini's death. He mentioned Dr. Moscatelli who had rowed round the edge of the harbour in a bumboat, had known Crabb well by sight and had described him accurately. Notari assured him that he was well known at least by name and description to many men of the Tenth Flotilla. It was a slack day in Leghorn harbour, and Crabb and Notari had a strange reunion dinner. Particularly they discussed the last attack upon Gibraltar when Notari's warhead had almost killed Petty Officer Bell.

Notari had tried to go south after the armistice to join the Allies, but had been forced to go into hiding from the Germans at Lucca. Having broken through the German lines, he wondered if Crabb would do something for him. In the north, Borghese was organ-

110

ising to fight for the Republicans. In the south Captain
Forza, who had preceded Borghese in command of the
Tenth, was recruiting other old members to fight on
the Allied side. Notari would esteem it a favour of an
old comrade-in-arms if Crabb would send him south.
'My dear chap,' Crabb said, 'I'll be delighted to help
you. Of course I'll make arrangements. But really, this
is becoming a most complicated war.'

Notari made it clear that Moscatelli, Tadini, Cella and
others who had attacked from the *Olterra* were still on
the enemy side. Crabb would be even more delighted
to meet these men, under favourable circumstances. He
was surprised to learn that he was well known to the
enemy. They knew his name, they knew how he handled
clearance diving. They appreciated his gesture in burying Visintini, but with booby-trapped mines they would
do their best to blow him apart. If he found such mines
he could try to cut off the section of the bilge keel with
underwater cutting gear and carry the mine with it.
Naval salvage officers taught him how to use the gear,
and he practised cutting plates beneath water. Whether
he could expertly burn round the side of a mine, without exploding it, was something which he would have
to find out when the time came.

Leghorn had been taken in July of 1944. Crabb steadily built up his defences. In October the front was still
only twenty miles to the north, and still the frogmen had
not acted. He knew in his bones that some day they

would attack this main supply port for the American forces in North-West Italy, but could no longer ignore a personal problem. When October had passed, he called upon the naval surgeon and said: 'The fact is . . . I have the most improbable complaint . . . actually it's piles.' He entrusted his team temporarily to another officer and went to hospital, just before the enemy came.

On a dark night in November, a British mine-watcher was walking along a breakwater. His task was to drop light charges into the water at intervals, and he had been dropping them night after night for months, killing an occasional fish. As he stopped to light another charge, he heard a cough from the concrete outcrop of the breakwater. He lit his charge, dropped it into the water and walked quietly away to warn the rest of the patrol. They came down silently with rifles, the mine-watcher pointed the direction and they fired into the concrete. From the darkness three men of the Gamma Group came out with their hands above their heads. The leading man was tall, his rubber suit was torn, and as they led him away he continued his interrupted coughing. They were tired, they stumbled in their weariness, but at first they refused to talk.

Leghorn echoed to the uproar of the bomb-disposal party's charges. Knowles, Venturini and Giari went over the side to search for mines among the American supply ships; the officer temporarily in command of the team was not a shallow-water diver. If they found mines they were to report them, and an officer would go down in standard diving-gear. For Knowles it was a strange experience to dive in an attack without Crabb. For Giari, it was a most extraordinary situation. Here he was, swimming around American ships at anchor in an Allied port, looking for mines placed by men of his old unit. Knowles had told him that charge-dropping would cease while they were searching; otherwise, the whole situation was startlingly like Gibraltar.

It was so like Gibraltar that Giari thought he heard a small charge go off in the water. Then another small charge dropped close to him, and he realised that he was not being troubled by his imagination. A fool of a sentry on the ship above him had ignored the order and was throwing charges at him. It was clear to Giari that if he surfaced and shouted in Italian anything might happen. A third charge dropped quite close. He felt a violent pain in the back. He surfaced and, once again, surrendered to the Allies. The sentry chose not to shoot, and Giari was hauled on board.

Meantime, in Navy House, intelligence and security officers interrogated the real prisoners with brilliant results. No mines had been placed; all the men who attacked had been taken prisoner. Knowles and Venturini were called off and Giari was taken to a sick bay.

The interrogation was prolonged and skilled. The Naval security officer had the prisoners separated at once in single cells, then he had them brought to him one by one for interrogation. The giant who had coughed, the leader of the frogmen, was first. The security officer looked at him and produced from the files the giant's own photograph and record. 'You are Malacarne,' he said. It was a positive statement; he had dossiers on all the enemy frogmen and he had been waiting for this moment for a long time. The bewildered plump frogman was marched in; he had already warned them that the mines he had towed were booby-trapped. His photograph was shown him: Sorgetti. The third man, the silent sullen one, was identified as Bertoncin.

Venturini was summoned to confront Malacarne. 'Malacarne?' he said. The prisoner looked down at him. 'Malacarne, no?'

'Malacarne, yes,' the other replied, and spat in Venturini's eye. When Venturini had gone, the angry Malacarne began to talk. The three saboteurs were checked and cross-questioned until a full picture emerged. They had been dropped by fast motor-boat off the port and they had swum in, each man towing a float with two of the new booby-trapped mines. Malacarne also towed a bag of neutral buoyancy which held civilian clothing for four men. They had intended, after swimming ashore in Leghorn, to hide the bag of clothing, then swim back to American ships to place the mines. Returning to the shore, they were to swim up a canal, put on the civilian clothing, hide their Gamma gear, and enter Leghorn in daylight to find themselves jobs and settle down. Each man carried 50,000 lire to tide him over. In the young moon of December, a fourth member of the party was to arrive with more mines and equipment. A permanent sabotage centre was to be set up in Leghorn. Malacarne and company were to be 'Italian labour' in Leghorn by day, while they fixed booby-trapped mines by night. It was an excellent idea and Malacarne had been understandably angry when he met the reception committee and his former comrade Venturini.

One more member of the sabotage party had still to arrive, a certain Lieutenant Pavone. From the information which Malacarne and his friends had given. Lieutenant Pavone was also to come in from the sea, towing equipment for further operations. A warm reception was arranged for him. The patrols and gate guards were warned to watch out for a man in overalls, wearing a certain type of boot. A saboteur when he landed could put overalls over his rubber suit, but could not diguise his boots.

At eight one morning in December, an American gate guard saw an Italian walking very wearily out of the gates, wearing overalls and the right type of boots. He called the Italian over, lifted one leg of the overalls and exposed the leg of a wet rubber suit. Enter Pavone.

115

The mines and equipment which he had towed were recovered from shallow water. So ended the assault upon Leghorn. If it had succeeded, similar sabotage centres were to have been established in almost every important port that the Allies held.

CHAPTER 8

ENTER BELLONI

KNOWLES knew that something was wrong. Since Crabb had left hospital he had been behaving in an odd fashion. He was extremely irritable. When a letter arrived with the stamp the wrong way round, the Monarch's head downwards, Crabb was furious. He said that it was a considered insult to the Crown. And then there was the incident of the horned mine. The mine, so thoroughly conventional in appearance and type that it was recognised by members of the public, had been washed ashore on a beach. To render it safe, Crabb had first to unbolt and open the horned shell. The cover nuts were rusty and he began to beat at them testily with a bomb spanner. Knowles was highly alarmed. Some way down the beach, fishermen had been watching. When the hammering began, and unmistakably strong language began to drift towards them, they disappeared like Arabs over the sand dunes. The hammering and cursing went on, and when Knowles could bear it no longer, he stood to attention and said crisply, 'Excuse me, sir. I'm going for a george.' He walked swiftly up the beach and got down out of sight behind cover. As he lay there, it occurred to him that it was just possible that Lieutenant-Commander Crabb was becoming bomb-happy. It happened to a lot of good men. There was no one with whom he could discuss the matter. He wouldn't pass the time of day with Sub-Lieutenant Venturini. Petty Officer Giari was out of sick bay, but Knowles didn't regard him as the man to know whether another man was all right in the head. He would have to stick by Crabb until the end. When the hammering ceased, he emerged from cover and behaved as if his officer was quite normal. He admired Crabb and he hated to see this happening to him.

Next day, they were ordered to fly to a quick job in the South of France. Shallow-water divers were in such great demand that the senior bomb-safety officer for Northern Italy had to deal with underwater mines in the harbour of Port Sète, to the east of Marseilles. When they arrived at the French airport Crabb had a roaring match with an American G.I. who did not recognise his uniform. Knowles reckoned that this was just his luck. Only a few days before Christmas, when he had planned a very special celebration in Leghorn with Giari and some friends, here he was in the South of France with the mistral blowing across the flat land and anything liable to happen. If he could believe what he saw in the papers, the war was almost over. He had thought that he was going to survive it, and here he was about to look for mines with Lieutenant-Commander Crabb off his nut.

The hotel in Port Sète had been badly bombed. There was no electric light. One thing Knowles had to admit was that the cognac was all right. On the afternoon of their arrival, he was having a second glass in a café on the quay, keeping a quiet eye on the Lieutenant-Commander, when Crabb suddenly shouted: 'Knowles, that cognac tastes terrible. Absolute bootleg stuff. I am giving you a direct order not to drink it. Do as I say, Knowles, or you'll end the war in irons.'

Knowles put down his glass. His suspicions were confirmed. He noticed that, besides everything else, his officer's face was a queer colour. He could report the whole thing to the Navy, of course, but he had to be careful. Liable to be charged with mutiny.

'Aye, aye, sir,' said Knowles.

On the morning before Christmas, they tackled the most difficult job. Germans had loaded a mine into the hull of a small motor-boat and had scuttled the craft alongside the quay in thirty feet of water. The mine could not be rendered safe under water. Nor could it be detonated where it lay without damaging the quay. Crabb cursed and fumed and was most ungenerous in his remarks about the Germans. Knowles laughed politely, but a little nervously. He was very relieved when he heard that the mine was not to be dealt with until the afternoon. Crabb said he was tired, and Knowles had never heard him say that before.

At lunch in the French naval mess, a French surgeon lieutenant-commander offered Crabb wine and he refused it. He said that somehow he had lost the taste for it. The surgeon shrugged. 'You are suffering from jaundice,' he said.

Crabb left the table hurriedly. He had not seen his face for days. With no lights and no mirrors in the hotel, he had shaved by touch. He looked in a mirror, saw that the surgeon was right, and wondered why the hell Knowles had said nothing about it. He couldn't understand Knowles these days. Damned fellow was behaving so secretively, acting like a lunatic. He decided to say nothing to him about jaundice. They still had this tricky mine to deal with and he didn't want to make Knowles nervous. In all his experience of him, the stoker had seemed afraid of nothing, but one never knew.

In the afternoon, they dived and fixed a hawser from the far side of the basin to the motor-boat. Then, operating a hand winch, they dragged the motor-boat with its mine inch by inch into the centre of the basin. Both Crabb and Knowles were uncommonly awkward with one another, each trying to put the other at his ease. When the motor-boat had been dragged into the center of the basin Crabb was exhausted, with his main job still to be done. He had to dive to the mine and fix a charge to be detonated from the shore. When the area was cleared, he dived, fixed the charge to the shell of the mine, then swam ashore, to sit shivering in the car, while another officer prepared to fire the charge. He saw fishermen in rowing-boats waiting for the explosion to row forward and collect the dead fish.

In the car, he heard a sound like an apologetic cough. Then the fury of the fishermen drifted towards him on the wind. He had mucked the job, and he began to appreciate how ill he was. Very wearily, he climbed out of the car and returned to his discarded DSEA set. He found that Knowles was also preparing to dive. 'Sir,' said Knowles, 'I thought perhaps you'd let me try. What with watching you and one thing and another, I think I can do it. Bit of extra experience, like.'

Crabb would cheerfully have allowed Knowles to dive, and to hell with the Director of Bomb Disposal. But the apologetic cough had been the sound of the detonating charge exploding on the shell of the mine. He could not allow Knowles to deal with a mine which was probably in a delicate state after such a treatment. When he went down again, he saw that the detonating charge had blown a hole in the side of the mine, leaving the main explosive intact. He placed his second charge on the explosive, surfaced, got ashore and waved to the detonating officer. The basin erupted. The fishermen, who had come a little nearer in their anxiety to collect dead fish, rowed for their lives.

The same afternoon Crabb went to hospital, and there he stayed for more than two months. When he felt a little better he began an exhausting war with the matron, who had classified his Picasso prints as pin-ups and ordered him to take them down. In his own interests, and in the interests of the hospital, several attempts were made to evacuate him to England, but he resisted them. He intended to be with the troops entering La Spezia. He wanted to meet the prisoners taken there, and he wanted to have a very close look at the Tenth Flotilla headquarters which had played so large a part in his life.

In March of 1945 he was allowed to go back to Leghorn, to go into hospital there. He reached Leghorn, ignored the hospital and set himself up in his old headquarters, the Villa Banti. It was a dull, bombed building of red brick which he had chosen with great care. The Villa Banti had a long drive, along which his shore bomb-disposal parties placed the mines and bombs which they had found and had rendered safe. In the Villa Banti they had a minimum of visits and interference from superior naval authority. There he could keep his teams intact and resist any attempt to have them dispersed in barracks. When the suggestion that they should all move into barracks had been made, he had taken the Maintenance Commander for a slow tour of the drive, had pointed out mines of particular interest and had asked politely where he intended to store the mines and bombs after the teams had gone. No more was heard of the move.

Returning to the Villa Banti, Crabb made a signal indicating that he was back in business. He was full of the delights of anticipation. The armies had been bogged down through the winter, like himself. They were now ready, as he was, to move up for La Spezia. He only needed confirmation from the Navy.

In reply to Crabb's signal, the Fleet Torpedo Officer ordered him to join the naval token force assembling at Ancona to enter Venice. He reckoned that the whole thing was a mistake and that the signal must have been corrupt and not properly decoded. He had no intention of going to Venice until after the war. He was no philistine: he had walked in the wonder of Rome, trying to share his joy with Knowles; Knowles had been inclined to agree with the soldier who said that Rome was a town with a smashing NAAFI. At any other time Crabb would have been very pleased to go to Venice. But now he had business to finish. He queried the signal and it was confirmed. He telephoned to Caserta, and was ordered to Venice in unmistakably plain and strong language. It slowly dawned on Crabb that he was still considered a sick man and was being rested.

Venice was not to be opened as a supply port for the

head of the Adriatic. Trieste would serve. While his teams went to La Spezia, Genoa and Trieste, he was to join the token force for Venice as bomb-safety officer. He knew that he deserved a rest, but he had no desire to be the Grand Old Man of clearance diving, aged thirty-five. Even Knowles was heading north-west without him.

Under another officer's command Knowles eventually reached Savona, on the north-west frontier of Italy, and was sent to find his own billet. Knowles drove Crabb's old truck up and down until he found a large villa with a flagstaff in the garden. He rapped on the villa's door.

"How many live here?" he asked of the man who opened the door.

"I live alone."

"Right. Well that's you and me living here now. You're the caretaker and this is the Royal Naval Barracks, Savona."

The Ensign on the truck was dusty. It had served with Crabb and Knowles for a very long time. The stoker took it from the truck, prepared to run it up in sunlight on the flagstaff in the garden. Stoker Sydney James Knowles B.E.M. removed his cap and ended his war.

Meantime, Crabb boarded a blood-bank plane for Ancona, where the naval token force for Venice was assembling. There were six officers and about a hundred ratings. Their commanding officer, Commander Backhouse, and his American second-in-command were extremely busy men. Backhouse appeared to be a man of few words. For the first few days, all Crabb heard him say was 'Good show' or 'Bad show'.

In the move-up for Venice, Backhouse vanished with the Army and it fell to Crabb to lead the token force in a convoy of trucks driven by Cypriots and guarded by Cypriot policemen. Backhouse had ordered him to ensure that the token force was a well-dressed party. He astonished his ratings by insisting that they enter Venice in Number One uniforms, with boots, belts and gaiters. On 29th April 1945, the 56th London Division entered Venice closely supported by Crabb and his well-dressed party.

They established a communications centre. Crabb went out to the Lido, and to his great embarrassment was asked to accept the surrender of an Italian Republican midget submarine. What the hell was he supposed to do with a midget submarine? He sent it to be moored at the Arsenal and handed the crew of five over to the Army, then got on with the job of taking over the mine stores on the Lido. He captured intact the controls for the controlled mine-field at the north-eastern entrance to the lagoon. 'Good show,' said Backhouse. The naval token force had no boat of their own, and to examine other naval installations they had to hire boats from the Army. 'Bad show,' said Backhouse.

Lieutenant Tony Marsloe of the U.S. Navy arrived and they had a drink together. Marsloe had been consistently following the scent of the Tenth Flotilla, and Crabb was inclined to envy him his job. After they had parted, he realised that he had forgotten to ask Marsloe why he was in Venice rather than La Spezia.

The officers of the token force were billeted in the Danieli Hotel, and when Crabb first arrived he was able to vent some of his wrath on the waiters who spoke to him in German. The waiters had served Germans a matter of hours before; they were accomplished linguists, but they found it difficult to keep track of the war. The naval party's stay in the Danieli was short, and when they moved out to find less imposing quarters, Crabb, as unofficial purser to the party—he was the only one with any money—was presented with a bill. It was a large bill, at peace-time rates. He took the bill to Backhouse, who said, 'Pay it, Crabb. We must keep our end up. We are a well-dressed party.'

While Crabb was engaged in paying bills, taking over submarines and checking sailors' lanyards, Marsloe had been talking to the Partisan liaison officer and to certain prisoners held in the Naval Academy of Venice. He vanished for the best part of the day, and returned in great excitement to look for Crabb.

To the north-east of the Lido lies the small island of Le Vignole. Discovering that the Republicans had used the island as a base for training German frogmen in piloted torpedoes, Marsloe had gone out there. The workshops and laboratories were intact, the island had a fascinating array of Tenth Flotilla equipment, and two bold sergeants of the Tenth Flotilla had stayed with it. They were wedded to their gear and they had refused to retreat with the Germans. They had decided that, whatever else happened, the gear should not fall into the hands of the Partisans. They had both once fought in Russia, and had some idea that the Partisans would hand over their precious equipment to the Russians. Marsloe had found the sergeants very friendly. They were quite willing to surrender to Anglo-American forces, but they would not surrender to the Partisans. How they had proposed to defend the island if the Partisans had decided to land was not quite clear.

Marsloe and Crabb set off for the island, entered the main canal of Le Vignole which almost cuts the island in two, and sailed to the torpedo workshops. Two Italians in shorts, without shirts, came down to the landing-stage to meet them. They introduced themselves as Sergeant Berni and Sergeant Fraguglia of the Tenth Flotilla. They were extremely tough-looking specimens, but they assured the officers of their good faith. They had heard of Crabb, and they rubbed their hands on their shorts and offered to shake hands. On the whole, they explained, they were glad to be rid of

127

the Germans. Under water, the Germans were very clumsy.

When civilities had been exchanged, the ex-enemy sergeants conducted the officers round the torpedo workshops, where the machines had been serviced. Just before they left, the Germans had taken the torpedoes out at dead of night and had hidden them in the canals. The sergeants had watched from cover and they were pretty certain that the Germans had placed the machines carefully, hoping to re-enter Venice as a sabotage party and to pilot the machines against Allied ships. But the sergeants believed that the Germans' technical knowledge was not equal to their intentions.

Berni and Fraguglia were anxious about their beloved torpedoes; they were afraid they would be ruined if they were left too long. They were deeply disappointed about the way the war was turning out in Europe, but they thought that if the machines were recovered in time they could be serviced and used against the Japanese. They explained that some of the torpedoes were of the new, faster San Bartolemo type, and it would be a shocking waste if they were never used in action. Crabb was slowly learning that most of the assault-craft operators of the Italian Tenth Flotilla had the political wisdom of an Apache war party.

As they walked round the laboratories the sergeants pointed out items of especial interest, as one frogman to another. Lieutenant-Commander Crabb had heard of

Commander Angelo Belloni, had he not? Crabb certainly had. Belloni was a first-world-war submariner and inventor who had conceived the whole idea of the Tenth Light Flotilla, invented much of its gear and persuaded Mussolini of its possibilities. The swimmers of the Gamma Group had worn Belloni diving-suits and Belloni breathing-gear. Belloni was Crabb's most important enemy.

The sergeants said that Commander Belloni had been in this very laboratory until the Germans retreated. They spoke as if they were speaking of the revered dead. Belloni, they said, was believed to have been captured by the Partisans; he had been known as a friend of Mussolini. It was a sticky end for a grand old man.

Berni and Fraguglia were officially taken prisoner and told to remain on the island, looking after the gear, until other arrangements could be made, while Crabb and Marsloe made best speed back to the main island. Marsloe could see no good reason why they shouldn't take over Le Vignole, assess the value of the equipment and the experiments which had been going on there, and then perhaps use the place to carry out experiments for their own navies. Crabb was not so sure that the Royal Navy would agree to it. He was just as enthusiastic as Marsloe, but he—not Marsloe—would have to sell the idea to Commander Backhouse.

The Commander puffed his pipe, and Crabb talked about the project through clouds of tobacco smoke.

When he had finished, Backhouse removed his pipe just long enough to say, 'Why not? My dear Crabb, you can carry on. This is my parish.'

They made a few discreet enquiries of the Partisan liaison officer about the untimely end of Commander Belloni. The Partisan liaison officer laughed. Partisans had surrounded the Venice Naval Academy and imprisoned Republican officers there. Commander Belloni had tried to stroll quietly away from the Academy in shorts and an open-necked shirt. He might have escaped but for the fact that he wore the badge of the Italian Tenth Flotilla on his wrist. He was not dead: he was in the local jail. 'My God,' said Crabb, 'we've got to get him out. So far as I'm concerned he's the most important prisoner of the war.'

CHAPTER 9

PRISONERS
AND
GENTLEMEN

THERE were two Bellonis in the same cell in the local jail—Commander Angelo, in his late sixties, and Signor Julio in his early teens. Julio Belloni having come to get his father out of jail, had been thrown in beside him. But Marsloe, who had been a New York attorney, talked them out of there and into the custody of the Allied Navies Experimental Station, Sant' Andrea. The Allied Navies involved were, of course, Crabb and himself; Sant' Andrea was the name of the fort on Le Vignole.

When they were some way from the prison, Marsloe told Julio to cut and run for home. Angelo Belloni did not seem at all surprised at his change of fortune. He talked to Marsloe quite affably. He was wearing the shirt and shorts in which he had been captured, and on his arm he still sported the badge of the Tenth Light Flotilla, a skull with a rose in its jaws, superimposed upon a figure X. He was a distinctive old man, with a shaven skull, and considering the ugly mood of the Partisans in Venice, Tony Marsloe did not want to tempt them. Crabb had returned to Sant' Andrea and Marsloe took Belloni there as quickly as possible.

The inventor was equally affable with Crabb. He had heard the name, he said; he'd had some quite good ideas to try out in Gibraltar, but never had a chance. Pity. One of Belloni's minor accomplishments was that he spoke idiomatic English in an extremely loud voice. He was very deaf, but he could lip-read English. Crabb had prepared a few choice words which he intended to say to Belloni, the man who had so affected his last two years but he found that his prisoner had no intention of letting him get a word in edgeways. Why, Belloni wanted to know, had English frogmen worn such a travesty of the Belloni diving-suit in their swimming attack upon Palermo? It was murder, said Belloni; you drowned them. Disgusting. It was clear to his captors that the old inventor was nether a diplomat nor a war historian. Such an unfounded allegation would hardly endear him to the Royal Navy.

It was clear that Belloni was not safe in Venice in the neighbourhood of either Partisans or British forces, but Marsloe and Crabb needed him to help them make full reports on all the gear. He spoke about the gear for several hours, and used the admiring sergeants Fraguglia and Berni to demonstrate specific points that he made. At last he was persuaded back into the launch to return to the main island with the Allied officers. Crabb wanted a guard for the workshops and equipment; he also wanted a guard for Belloni.

In the launch the old man continued to talk diving, drew Crabb out by questions, then shouted his own opinions with emphatic gestures, sitting still only when he had to lip-read the replies. From the far side of the canal of Le Vignole, a girl began to wave. Belloni saw her and mentioned casually that the girl was his daughter, Minella. Julio must have told her that he was on Le Vignole he said, it was just like Minella to land on the wrong side of the island. As the launch turned back to pick up his anxious daughter, Belloni resumed his interrupted flow of diving talk.

Minella was a striking girl of about eighteen. As she settled in the launch, she gazed at the English and American uniforms with hatred. Belloni apologised for his daughter and explained that she and her elder sisters Paola and Maura had been serving with the Tenth Flotilla, in the Italian equivalent of the Wrens or the Waves. Then he and his daughter began a spirited conversation, ignoring the others, which lasted till they reached Venice. Minella was convinced that her father had the situation in hand.

133

Commander Backhouse was delighted to see Belloni. He agreed that the old man should remain on the island until the intelligence work was completed and he released Chief Petty Officer Canning from the naval token force to look after Belloni. The C.P.O. was redhaired and kindly, and within a very short time Belloni was calling him 'Ginger—my nurse'. A platoon of Polish soldiers was alloted to guard the island.

Crabb, Marsloe, Belloni, Canning and the two Italian sergeants were preparing to take up quarters in the Forte Sant' Andrea, when a most important signal was received. Because of the political situation in Yugoslavia, Trieste could not serve as a supply port for the head of the Adriatic. Venice, instead, would have to be cleared of mines and opened swiftly.

Minesweepers, making their slow and dangerous way in from the sea, dared not explode mines which were lying close in-shore, and so risk severely damaging important installations and places of historical interest. Crabb was not only Bomb Safety Officer. He was the only Allied shallow-water diver in the area, suddenly faced with the largest mine-clearance job of his career.

Sergeants Berni and Fraguglia had served in Abyssinia and in Spain, with the Italian Blue Division in Russia, and in the Tenth Flotilla. One war was very much like another, in their opinion. They were trained divers and they volunteered to help Crabb clear Venice of German mines. Belloni improved upon the plan. Held as prisoners by the Partisans in the Naval Academy, he said, were a number of Tenth Flotilla officers and petty officers who had been helping to train Germans in assault craft before they were captured. There were a number of excellent divers amongst them, said Belloni, and he began to recite the list from memory. Only two of the names meant anything to Crabb, but those names meant a great deal. Dr. Moscatelli, formerly surgeon and captain of the *Olterra*, was amongst them, and so was Lieutenant Tadini who had sunk two ships at Gibraltar in the piloted-torpedo attacks of May and August 1943. Belloni felt that they would be only too happy to do a little bit of clearance diving, if it meant getting out of the way of the Partisans.

Marsloe put the proposition to the Partisans and they agreed. Being blown up by mines was all that officers of the Tenth Flotilla were fit for, the Partisan commander said. Marsloe was allowed to choose his men and take them under escort to Le Vignole. Commander Backhouse, having committed himself to the idea of Le Vignole in the first place, boldly agreed. Crabb was beginning to appreciate Commander Backhouse. The prisoners were brought under escort to Le Vignole, and Belloni introduced them one by one. Dr. Moscatelli, a dark, stocky man, shook Crabb's hand warmly. 'I remember you well from Gibraltar,' he said, 'but why

135

did you shave off your beard?' He introduced Lieutenant Tadini.

The rest of the prisoners were far from happy. They had no idea what they were in for, except that it involved mine clearance. They had heard that certain of their enemies considered it fit and proper to march their prisoners over mine fields until they found the mines.

Crabb pointed out to them that the war was virtually over, but the mines in the canals of Venice had not been located. It was, of course, one thing to place a limpet mine, and quite another to search for German ground mines which they did not understand. Some of them might not care for the work. If any of them felt that they were not up to the job, he would return them to the Partisans, who, he fully expected, would give them all the privileges normally accorded to prisoners of war. On the other hand, if they chose to stay and help he would see that they were properly housed and fed, he would allow them as much latitude as possible and would try to put them in touch with their families.

A heated discussion followed. One prisoner said that he had heard of this Crabb who had buried the great Visintini, but he had killed Visintini in the first place, had he not? Another pointed out that there was nothing dishonourable in taking German mines from the canals of Venice; what right had the Germans to mine Venice? Moscatelli ended the discussion by announcing simply, 'We will stay.'

Crabb had, on paper, the most imposing local clearance-diving party of the Italian compaign. The senior appointments of the Royal Naval Clearance Diving Team, Venice, were Lieutenant-Commander Crabb, R.N.V.R., commanding; Lieutenant-Commander Marsloe, U.S.N.R., liaison and 2 i/c; Commander Belloni, adviser on equipment; Surgeon Moscatelli, doctor and senior diver. With Tadini, the Italian sergeants and the other prisoners, he had eight more divers.

He had one more matter to clear up, and he made a speech to his new staff after he had given it thought.

'Gentlemen,' he said, and the prisoners looked surprised when the word was translated, 'I don't know whether you are officially prisoners of war, escaped prisoners of war, surrendered personnel or what you are. This will have to be clarified. I have only a platoon of Polish soldiers, who are fully engaged guarding the workshops. I cannot guard you. Gentlemen, I must ask for your word of honour that you will not try to escape.'

Some of the Italians knew that they would have sooner or later to face trial for fighting on the Republican side against the legal government of Italy. They could easily swim away from Le Vignole, but they gave their word that they would not escape, and no man broke it.

Since the Italian prisoners were not officially on the island, they could not be officially fed but Pro-Allied Italians at a Royal Army Service Corps ration point proved most helpful and sympathetic. The prisoners were housed in the Forte Sant' Andrea. Using Belloni gear, the team began work on the following morning.

The controlled mine-field lay in the north-eastern entrance to the lagoon. Although the controls had been removed, there was no guarantee that the mines could not be operated by some alternative method. Mine-sweepers could not deal with this type of mine. The team dived for the mines, which lay in sixty feet of water, twice the maximum depth at which their breathing gear was considered safe. When the mine-field was cleared, they concentrated on Venice.

The Germans had sown their entire stock of ground mines just before they left, and two of the mines had been reported close to the cruiser moorings off the junction of the Giadecca and the Grand canals. If mine-sweepers flushed mines there, the explosion could easily affect St. Mark's Square, the church of St. Mark's and the Doge's Palace. The team dived repeatedly in search of mines round the cruiser buoys and found none. They turned to searching for mines close to the quays and harbour installations of the old port.

A magnetic-acoustic mine had been reported in the vicinity of a brand-new Italian tanker which had been used by the Germans as a reservoir for fresh water in case the advancing Allies cut supplies. The tanker was squatting with her bottom in the mud, a hundred yards from a quay. If there was a magnetic-acoustic mine there, it would explode the moment the tanker floated and started her engines. A minesweeper could not explode it without blowing up the tanker.

Crabb tried to impress upon the Italians that, since they wore metal oxygen canisters and had none of the special non-magnetic gear which is considered essential in diving for magnetic mines, they went in danger of their lives. The Italians were not fully convinced that he was not trying to frighten them for the fun of it. They had already observed that Lieutenant-Commander Crabb had an unusual sense of humour.

He gave them an example in the hope of proving his point. In the South of France a United States naval diver of an underwater demolition team had been sent down to find a magnetic mine. He was wearing conventional deep-diving gear, including lead-soled shoes. He found the mine; it destroyed both him and his attendants on the surface. The Italians observed that this was extremely sad, and still looked at Crabb with suspicion. He was wearing the same diving-gear as they were. Anything an English diver could do was certainly well within their powers. The Tenth Flotilla had always taught its men to have a high opinion of themselves.

For the sake of the tanker, Crabb chose to dive alone. The water, as is usual in Venice, was filthy and dark. As he searched close to the bottom, thirty feet out from the tanker's side, he scraped over an obstruction. He examined the obstruction, and headed straight for the surface. It had been an eerie experience in dark water to touch the tail of a magnetic-acoustic mine. He marked the spot and boarded the tanker. He told the captain that there *was* a mine, but that there was no need to worry or to evacuate his ship so long as no machinery was started.

All but the tail of the mine was buried in the mud and he hadn't a hope of rendering it safe under water. The bright German who had placed the mine had calculated that it could not be exploded without taking the tanker with it, and the tanker could not be moved without exploding the mine. The harbour had to be cleared, and the stake in the game was a new tanker of over ten thousand tons.

Crabb considered that it would be possible to place a charge on the mine and blow the tail unit, with its firing mechanism, from the mine without exploding the main charge; but Crabb had never tried this, and he had no desire to begin experimenting hard by a tanker. In the main canal at Le Vignole, two similar mines had been reported and ignored until now, under the pressure of more important work. He decided to find one of them and try an experimental demolition. The team went back to Le Vignole and he set the Italians diving in search of the mines.

While they spread out along the canal and began diving in the dirty water, he wandered along the bank and came upon a cache of arms, revolvers, tommy-guns and ammunition, all tidily wrapped in oiled cloths, evidently by old and experienced soldiers. He had a very good idea who the soldiers were. The sergeants Berni and Fraguglia had maintained that the Germans had removed all the arms and ammunition from Le Vignole. He had never believed that the bold sergeants intended to defend the island against Partisans with their bare hands, but until now he had no evidence of arms. Berni and Fraguglia were like foxes, and like foxes they would have alternative dens stocked with supplies, for moon-light flittings. He wondered how many caches of arms there were on Le Vignole, and he began to make a mental inventory of the weapons he had found. Time passed. He heard someone shout. He left the cache of arms and walked along the bank till he came in sight of the divers.

An Italian swimmer was bobbing up and down in the water in great excitement, shouting that he had found a mine. As he surfaced and shouted, dived, surfaced and shouted again, his metal oxygen canisters were quivering. Crabb ordered to him to come ashore at once, before he ruined the mine. The remark was translated and the prisoners thought it funny. When the Italian was well away from the mine, Crabb dived. The mine was similar to the one he had found by the tanker. He came ashore for the charge which he had prepared, fixed it to the mine and again came ashore to

141

fire the charge by remote control. It worked: the tail unit was blown off without affecting the main explosive.

With a second charge, he prepared to return to the tanker. Before he fired that charge, he intended to have the tanker evacuated and the area cleared. With luck, he could blow off another tail unit. Without luck, the Italians would be short of a tanker and, possibly, a section of the quay of the old port of Venice. He had to hurry back, for four hours had passed in the search and the experiments. The matter of the secret store of arms would have to be left until later.

Meantime, the captain of the tanker was about to explode the mine. He could not think what had kept the English officer. He could refloat his ship without using any machinery, and he decided to do it. It would move his ship a little farther from the mine in the mud, and it would probably save a little time. He opened his sea-cocks and let his supply of fresh water pour out. The mine was between his ship and the quay. It did not occur to him that by floating the tanker he would alter the magnetic field between the tanker and the quay, and so explode the mine. The moment the tanker floated, the mine exploded. The tanker continued to float, and no damage was done to the quay. The mine was buried so deeply in the mud that the mud absorbed most of the explosion.

The Bomb Safety Officer returned to find the whole thing over. He dived to examine the tanker and found only a dent in a plate. He was extremely relieved that he would not now have to put his experiment to the test, and he was more than cordial to the captain. When the captain remarked that magnetic mines were less dangerous than he had been given to believe, Crabb agreed. He was sitting in the captain's cabin with a glass of excellent wine. He said, 'Oh, quite; magnetic mines are noisy, that's all.'

He was in an excellent humour in the launch as the team journeyed back to Le Vignole. To the Italians' great surprise, he paraded them before the Forte Sant' Andrea and suggested that each prisoner who had hidden firearms should collect them and hand them over to Chief Petty Officer Canning. He pointed out that an armed prisoner of war was not very closely protected by the Geneva Conventions, and he looked sadly, as he talked, at Fraguglia and Berni.

It had also been brought to his attention, he said, that Lieutenant Tadini was in the habit of leaving his room in the Forte Sant' Andrea after dark and swimming away from the island to join his girl friend in Venice. In future, when Lieutenant Tadini was irresistibly compelled to Venice, he would ask permission, and, if granted permission, would proceed by ferry, to preserve the dignity of the Royal Naval Clearance Diving Team. If Lieutenant Tadini should meet a Partisan patrol in Venice, the Royal Navy would inform his next-of-kin.

He dismissed them, and within an hour Canning had a large stock of small arms and ammunition. Crabb was treating the prisoners as he had treated his Underwater Working Party in Gibraltar. If his gamble succeeded, if they worked really well, he could do his share of the clearance of Venice very quickly. If the gamble failed, he might be court-martialled, but he did not believe that he had any choice in the matter. He could lead the Italians but he could not drive them. He had to let them keep a little pride and help them to maintain the idea that they were clearing up Venice for the sake of Venice and not for the sake of Anglo-American forces. If they were to be disciplined, they would have to be disciplined by a fellow-Italian. So far that Italian had not emerged.

On an early night in May, the minesweepers fired blanks in the harbour. There was Victory in Europe, and Venice rejoiced. In the morning St. Mark's Square was deep in sand. The Venetians had torn down the sandbags from the church of St. Mark's and the Doge's Palace and emptied them into the square.

As the clearance-diving team carried on, they began to work on the canal which joined Venice to the mainland port of Marghera. The canal is four miles long with an average width of two hundred feet. If one sizeable ship were sunk in the Marghera canal, the flow of traffic would be stopped or, at best, most seriously interrupted. The first quick flush of the canal revealed nothing, and a thorough search had to be made. The system was to have wires stretched taut along both banks of the canal, more than thirty feet beneath the surface (the canal has an average depth of thirty-three feet.) Between the parallel wires a cross-wire ran. The diver crawled along in the mud holding the cross-wire in one hand while he searched with his free hand. It was very dark below. When the diver had made one crossing of the mud from bank to bank, the cross-wire was moved forward a few feet and he repeated the journey from the other bank, searching another breadth of the bottom. When one man was exhausted, another took his place. Crabb was surprised to find how well the Italians worked. They had been used to attack, then to be fêted and to rest, before another glorious assault. There was no relief and no glorious victory to be won, in the mud of the Marghera.

Besides underwater mines, there were unexploded bombs to deal with, and destruction charges to be removed from vital points in the harbour. When his bomb-disposal team from Trieste arrived, Crabb felt that a siege had been raised. At Trieste, Lieutenant Joe Howard, R.N.V.R., and Lieutenant Gerald Shirley, R.N.V.R., had made a first flush of the danger points in three days, working against time to allow a British cruiser to enter harbour. They were trained divers and they had followed thousands of feet of cable to trace all but two mines of a large, dispersed controlled minefield. All but two was not enough for Howard. With visions of the cruiser blowing up, he searched doggedly for the mines until he could wait no longer. He determined to use the controls to blow up the hidden mines. He pressed the switches and the mines exploded—*on land*. An expensive section of mole slid gracefully into the harbour of Trieste. Ruefully he called the debris Howard's Folly.

Howard had been decorated for a particularly cool job on a beach-head. Twelve unexploded aerial torpedoes of unusual design had lain in the path of advance. The officer who rendered safe the first torpedo was killed by the second. Howard dealt with the remaining ten.

Gerald Shirley, with Howard as his deputy, had cleared a canal from Ravenna to the sea, making what their superiors termed a house-to-house collection of mines. German snipers had interfered with the work, until Howard complained to his own Army. As he explained, he and Shirley had only to put their heads above the canal bank to get air-conditioned.

They were good, cool men, and Crabb was delighted to have them in Venice. They set to work on the bombs and destruction charges, ably assisted by Howard's Knowles, one Able Seaman James R. Potts, who was to survive to run the helter-skelter at Southend.

When Crabb encountered a problem with no easy solution, he called upon Howard for advice. The problem consisted of two torpedo warheads placed with detonators in the mud beneath a bridge. 'How,' he asked Howard, 'should I render this safe?'

Joe Howard, a Glaswegian who believed in speaking his mind, hated to watch other men at work—the hallmark of a good bomb-safety officer. 'What do you mean, *render it safe*?' he asked. 'The very idea makes me sweat bottles of Bluebell. My advice to you, sir, is to blow the bloody thing up. What is another bridge in Venice?'

Crabb rendered it safe. He was growing fond of the bridges of Venice.

CHAPTER 10

SANT' ANDREA

ON LE VIGNOLE, much could be learned about underwater warfare at very little expense. The equipment had belonged to Italian Republican forces and the technical assistants were unpaid Italian prisoners. The Fleet Torpedo Officer authorised Crabb to learn what he could and make whatever experiments seemed necessary, pending the arrival of the Superintendent of Diving. Marsloe and he were to communicate the results to the Royal and United States Navies from their establishment, styled the Allied Navies Experimental Station, Sant' Andrea.

Angelo Belloni continued his experiments, closely watched. Like Sergeants Berni and Fraguglia, the elderly commander was becoming absorbed in the possibilities of the war against Japan, and he wanted to try out an idea which he had originally intended for the war against America. As early as 1942, the Tenth Flotilla had had a pocket submarine of advanced design, twelve tons in weight, carrying two men and two torpedoes. It was known as the CA, and it could be released from the deck of a parent submarine. Extensive training had begun in order that an ocean-going submarine lying before New York could release a pocket submarine to penetrate and sink shipping in the Hudson in December 1943. The attack was not to be simply a naval action. It was intended as a gesture, a thumb to the nose.

Foiled by the Italian armistice, Belloni now entreated Crabb and Marsloe to persuade their navies to use the pocket submarine against Japan. By all accounts the Japanese had tried hard to use midget submarines; Belloni proposed that they should be shown how to use them properly. The Royal and United States Navies, with midget submarines of their own, showed no wild enthusiasm, but Belloni did not take offence. He continued working.

The Allied Navies were much more interested in his experiments with mixture gases for breathing apparatus. The Royal Navy let him have an Italian decompression chamber which they had acquired, and the U.S. Navy arranged a supply of helium from their blimps which were working with British minesweepers at Venice. Belloni, beside himself with delight, began to work all hours of the night. He thought nothing of wakening Crabb at four in the morning to discuss an idea. Before the diving day began, Crabb and Marsloe had breakfast with Belloni, Moscatelli, Tadini and the other Italian officers. Breakfast with Belloni became an ordeal. By seven in the morning, the old man was often half-way through his working day and shouting the results of his experiments at the top of his voice. Chief Petty Officer Canning intervened: 'Sir,' he said to Crabb, 'the noise is coming straight through the partition. Commander Belloni is upsetting the kitchen staff. If I may suggest it, sir, it could be arranged that all officers have breakfast in their rooms.' Crabb was most happy to agree. The old man was exhausting himself and all around him.

For years, his eldest daughter Paola, a medical student, had acted as his secretary and had looked after him. The Allied Naval Experimental Station decided to employ her officially as a secretary, to carry on the work. Belloni raised no objections. He promised to teach Paola to speak English. When she arrived, Belloni greeted her affectionately, then handed her a copy of his diving manual which had been translated into English. 'Learn English from that,' he ordered, and she obeyed.

Meantime, Sergeants Fraguglia and Berni continued to mourn for the piloted torpedoes which the Germans had hidden. Two were of the new San Bartolemo type and of interest to Anglo-American intelligence services, but this was not exactly what Berni and Fraguglia had in mind. Since pro-Allied Italian assault swimmers had been used to attack German targets in the harbour of Genoa, Berni and Fraguglia expected to be called upon to pilot San Bartolemo torpedoes against the Japanese. So did Lieutenant Tadini.

They were encouraged by the recent history of Lieutenant de La Penne, who had disabled the *Valiant* at Alexandria in 1941 and had been sent to a prisoner-of-war camp. Returning a free man after the Italian armistice, de La Penne had called upon the Flag Officer Taranto, Vice-Admiral Sir Charles Morgan, formerly captain of the *Valiant*. Lieutenant de La Penne offered Sir Charles an apology for his silence on the night the *Valiant* was struck. His warhead had been in the mud, below the battleship, he explained. If he had talked too soon, it would have been a simple matter for the captain to have moved his ship away from it. Now, de La Penne suggested, they should let bygones be bygones, and he asked Sir Charles for a job. Sent against the Germans, de La Penne performed valiantly, and Admiral Morgan asked for a British decoration for him. The decoration was refused, but de La Penne was awarded an Italian medal, and Sir Charles Morgan, late of the *Valiant*, pinned it on his chest.

The Italians on Le Vignole reasoned that if all that could happen to their old comrade de La Penne, they had a fair chance of being sent against the Japanese.

151

Neither Crabb nor Marsloe argued the point, for they had to sustain the Italians' interest in the hidden piloted torpedoes. As soon as the task of clearing mines from the canals allowed, Crabb intended to have the torpedoes salvaged. The first flush for mines had been completed, and if he could find an Italian who could keep the others steadily at routine work, he could concentrate upon more interesting projects.

There had been one man in the Tenth Flotilla who could be depended upon to keep others at work. This was Lieutenant Eugenio Wolk, who had trained the Gamma Group. All the Italians at Sant' Andrea had been aware of the weight of Wolk's authority, and some of them had been aware of the weight of his fist. He was six foot four inches tall and an Olympic swimmer. Wolk had been the driving influence behind the enemy swimming attacks after the Italian armistice and had stuck by the Germans until almost the end. Then, when they robbed the remnants of his Gamma Group of their equipment and their initiative, Wolk had taken his men up into the mountains and had waylaid German trucks to provide them with food and ammunition, while he carried on a war against the Allies. Having served Italy in his fashion, Wolk had then disappeared.

In their first days at Sant' Andrea, Moscatelli and the others had talked a great deal about Wolk. His name was suddenly dropped from conversation, and Crabb and Marsloe wondered if they had heard something of

him, through contacts in Venice. They never ceased
to be surprised at how well the members of the Tenth
Flotilla kept in touch. In Leghorn, for example, Commander Notari had contacted Giari before he asked for
Crabb. In Venice Fraguglia and Berni had put them on
the track of Belloni, and Belloni had suggested the
others.

Crabb and Marsloe let it be known that they considered it was a pity that Wolk was on the run and that
he would be far better employed at Sant' Andrea. He
would have to stand trial, of course, but until he was
tried he could be free among his old comrades.

Before the end of May 1945, Captain Forza rang
and asked if Crabb would join him for a drink in Venice.
Forza had led the pro-Allied Italian swimmers and
assault-craft operators, and he was, in theory, an enemy
of Wolk. When Crabb joined him in the lounge of an
hotel, Forza asked him if he had any news of Wolk,
and Crabb said that he had not. He wished he had: he
could use him at Sant' Andrea. Forza signalled to a
man in civilian clothing at the next table. The civilian
came over to them. He was extremely tall, his civilian
clothes were ill-fitting and he wore spectacles. 'Lieutenant-Commander Crabb—Lieutenant Wolk,' said
Captain Forza. The introduction was being arranged
on the highest dramatic level of the Tenth Flotilla, and
Crabb rose to the occasion. 'Look here, you'd better
be my prisoner. But do sit down. What will you drink?'

Wolk had been in hiding in Venice for some time. He had contacted the prisoners of Le Vignole through their friends and relatives in Venice. When the offer of a job reached him he had decided to accept it, but not before he was properly introduced through a senior serving Italian naval officer. Captain Forza and he had known each other too well to let politics interfere with friendship.

Tony Marsloe, as usual, had to persuade the authorities that Wolk would be more useful on Le Vignole, under proper guard of course, than he would be in prison, but Marsloe decided that it would be tactless to say that the new prisoner was guarded by his promise not to escape.

Wolk resumed his authority over the other prisoners as though he had never been away, and mine clearance proceeded at a brisker pace. Shortly after his arrival, a second round-up of hidden revolvers and ammunition was arranged. By some strange chance, he explained, certain prisoners had quite forgotten to hand their weapons over. Wolk, far more successfully than the British and Americans, persuaded his old comrades that Sant' Andrea was not a home of rest for frogmen.

It was soon possible to divert a few of the prisoners from mine clearance to search for and to salvage the piloted torpedoes hidden in canals. Two San Bartolemos and three of the older slow-speed piloted torpedoes were brought to the surface, and arrangements were made

154

for mechanics to come from Milan to service them. Milan, where Mussolini had hung head downwards in a market square, was Communist-dominated, and the mechanics arrived wearing Communist badges. They had to share a mess with sergeants and petty officers of the Tenth Flotilla, and Crabb issued the highly optimistic order that there should be no discussion of politics at meals or at work. But both workmen and prisoners were piloted-torpedo enthusiasts first and politically-minded afterwards. In the workshops they laboured together on the machines for eleven hours a day six days a week. On Sundays they went as separate groups to the chapel of Sant' Andrea.

When the wet trials of the piloted torpedoes began, the Italians were most surprised to discover that the English officer could, and did, pilot the machines. Crabb mentioned Emily, the piloted torpedo which had been salvaged from the *Olterra*, but they were not satisfied with this. In the Tenth Flotilla torpedo pilots had been very carefully selected and given a year's training. How had he learned to pilot Emily? He explained shortly: 'With advice from a good torpedo engineer officer . . . and by fiddling.'

Talking of Emily reminded him of the morning in September 1943 when the *Olterra* was towed in and he thought the Italian affair was over. Since then Giari had served under him and Notari had asked for help. Now Moscatelli and Tadini, also from the *Olterra*, were working for him with Wolk who had trained the Gamma Group, and Belloni who had fathered the whole idea. He even knew how to lay hands on Sub-Lieutenant Cella, the only man who had escaped after Visintini's attack. Cella was keeping out of the way as an engineering student in Milan. Remembering the night in December 1942 when six Italians had set out and all but Cella had been killed or captured, Crabb let him be.

'There is one other person you must meet,' Wolk said; 'Signora Visintini.' He and Visintini had been close friends, and he said that Signora Visintini wanted to meet Crabb, to hear for herself how her husband had died and how he had been buried.

With Wolk, Crabb called upon Maria Visintini, who was living with her husband's mother in some rooms in an old palace on the Grand Canal. She was a handsome young woman, dressed in black, wearing no make-up, her fair hair tightly drawn back. She said very little. Wolk tried to make conversation but it tailed off. Visintini's mother asked Crabb a few questions and thanked him for coming. He returned to the Forte Sant' Andrea, and the memory of the meeting weighed on him.

Maria Visintini spoke English and had had secretarial training. She had become poor, and it occurred to him that he might offer her a job. He tried to dismiss the idea, but it refused to be dismissed, and he mentioned it to Wolk, who did not think it fantastic. Shortly afterwards, Wolk came into his office and said that

Signora Maria Visintini had landed. Would Crab first read the letter which she had written and had brought with her? It was in English, penned on both sides of a single sheet.

I was told by Wolk that there has been a proposal that I can work for you. He spoke to me about this.

I appreciate your thinking about me and your delicacy not to speak to me directly.

I have accepted and now it is I who want to speak to you. I need working. If you will give me the possibility of working with you, I'll thank you very much.

Life demands often sacrifices harder than death. To face them to win them, I think that this is courage. Especially if one is alone, a woman and she must live in a world that is not her own.

I don't say this only for you. It is all the Italian world that is no more as mine own was. As my husband's was. . . .

Now everything is dead and it is very strange that I'm speaking so just with you. May I think it be rightly understood by you? Life goes on. One must go on with life trying to be plucky and honest. Heart is a secret precious thing that can be seen by nobody. I need working. My husband's spirit from his heaven of peace sees in my heart and he can't but approve me. (This is for your peace of mind.) My pride and his was, is to show you how much Italian people can value. This is my strength and my consolation. (And this is the promise for my well to do work.) Now I'm very grateful for you to give me the possibility of work among you rather than otherwhere and so I've come to hear your conditions.

Crabb read the pages several times. Some time passed before he realised that Maria Visintini was still waiting outside. When she came in he asked her if she would become secretary to Marsloe and himself. They broke the strain by discussing the hours which she would work and by going into the petty detail of the office routine. Maria Visintini was to prove a very efficient secretary.

In a shallow patch by the north-east entrance of the lagoon a mine had been reported. Minesweepers had repeatedly swept the area and divers had searched time and again, without result. The shallow patch, which could be seen from the upper windows of the Forte Sant' Andrea, was off the main shipping channel and ships were warned to avoid it. On a quiet evening, Crabb saw an Italian coaster suddenly swing into the shallow patch, taking a short cut, ignoring the warning buoys. Before he could get downstairs, the coaster found the missing mine and began to go down by the head. The launch from Le Vignole took off the injured and the dead.

Peace was slow to come to Venice, but it arrived there before it reached many Italian cities. Venice suffered less from the hunger and anger and blood-letting which follows war and civil war. Meantime, the Venice Underwater Working Party continued to mop up mines on installations and in canals. They continued at full stretch, dividing their men and time between mine clearance and the experimental work.

When the minesweepers fired blanks in the harbour again and Crabb phoned Navy House to find what the beastly row was all about, he was told that there was victory in Asia.

There were many happy endings at Sant' Andrea. Lieutenant Gerald Shirley married an English nurse in Venice and Crabb was their best man. Belloni, Wolk, Moscatelli and Tadini stood trial before an Italian court for fighting on the Republican side, but their work in the mine-fields of Venice was taken into consideration and they were discharged—to return to Sant' Andrea and carry on the work. At the end of the war, the exact status of the prisoners had still to be defined. They continued without official rations and without pay. Crabb found himself becoming more and more of a welfare officer, trying to trace the prisoners' possessions, arranging visits by their wives. He and Marsloe had also to find money from their own pockets for cigarettes and wine.

As the tension relaxed, Wolk took a flat on the Lido for his wife, Tadini gave up the pretence of living in his room in the Forte Sant' Andrea while Belloni tried in vain to persuade the Allied Navies to get him a disarmed submarine to carry out certain experiments he had in mind.

159

In September the Italians on the island arranged a party which went with a swing, and when it was at its height they produced a brass crown they had made in the torpedo workshops and crowned Crabb king of Sant' Andrea. Commander W. O. Shelford, R.N., Superintendent of Diving for the Royal Navy, visited the island. He was enthusiastic about what he saw and he ordered that the experiments should continue.

But the Allied Navies Experimental Station was beginning to break up. An American military police officer arrived in a blaze of blanco with a heavily armed escort to take away Tadini, Fraguglia and Berni to demonstrate piloted torpedoes in the United States. Tony Marsloe persuaded the police officer to go away until Crabb and he could talk the three charioteers into volunteering for the trip. Having the interests of the United States Navy at heart, Marsloe knew full well that any demonstrations which Tadini, Fraguglia and Berni were *forced* to make would end in disaster. They left for the United States without handcuffs and reported in due course that they were having a whale of a time. Tony Marsloe himself was called away, and he came back only to marry Minella Belloni and to take her home to New York.

December often proved an eventful month for Crabb. Just before Christmas of 1945, he was temporarily relieved at Sant' Andrea and ordered to fly to Naples with his diving-gear. In Naples he was briefed by Sir

John Cunningham, the Commander-in-Chief Mediterranean, who began by explaining the situation in Israel.

Jewish underground organisations were determined to rid Israel of the British. Large British police launches had been blown up by underwater mines. Crabb was to fly to Haifa on Air Priority One to form an underwater working party there as he had formed parties in Gibraltar and in Leghorn. If he could not get a plane for Haifa straight away, Sir John would send him in his own Beaufighter.

Just after he arrived in Israel, his award of the O.B.E. was announced. He formed a diving team, and trained a party on each naval ship, sufficiently well to be able to examine the keel of their ship and to take a mine off in an emergency. Temporarily there was a lull in underwater sabotage, he went back to Italy under orders to hand over Le Vignole to the Italian Navy and to return to Haifa as soon as possible.

At the Forte Sant' Andrea there was a final party for all hands. Crabb destroyed the warheads of the piloted torpedoes, and they burned with a white flame which brought the launches of the Venice Fire Brigade on a false alarm. Then he ceremonially handed over Le Vignole to four captains of the Italian Navy. *A certain Commander Ernesto Notari* was to command the island.

CHAPTER 11

WHEN
THIS WAR
IS OVER

HAIFA became hot and violent. In the port were men of the 6th Airborne Division who had gone down west of the Orne on D Day and jumped low through the flak on the Rhine. In Europe they had been known as liberators; in Israel they were called British oppressors, and they sometimes carried shields to protect themselves from bricks and cricket boxes to protect themselves from hatpins. For the parachutists it was all very confusing, and on the march they often sang:

> *When this war is over*
> *Oh, how happy we shall be . . .*

On his first visit to Haifa, Crabb had lived in a hotel which was made nervous by whispers. In the front lounge a sheikh met visitors at odd hours, by appointment, sitting with his back to the wall. He was suspected of selling land to Jewish settlers. When Crabb returned, the sheikh had been assassinated, the hotel and much of Haifa was out of bounds, and naval officers slept behind one of the many knitted patterns of barbed wire.

Ships in the harbour were sometimes mined by saboteurs. Beyond that, it was not a war which Crabb understood at all.

One incident, though, did remind him of Gibraltar. An intelligence report that mines were about to be used against naval ships coincided with the loss of 900 yards of cable. This was too much of a coincidence for Captain destroyers, the bold and unconventional Captain J. H. Ruck Keene, R.N., O.B.E., D.S.C. Soldiers and policemen searched around on the moles and found nothing, and Crabb with his clearance-diving team swam round in a general search of the harbour. The morning wore on, and Crabb dived with diminishing hope until he was ordered to report immediately to Ruck Keene. He liked Ruck Keene, he feared Ruck Keene and he had nothing to report, but he paraded aboard H.M.S. *Chequers* in his swimming-trunks. The word 'immediately' had no shades of meaning for Ruck Keene. 'Ha,' said the captain, 'pour yourself a drink before you fall down.' From the instruments and charts on his desk, it was obvious that Captain D. had also been exploring. He said that he was right in thinking, was he not, that a saboteur could explode a home-made mine by remote control? The saboteur could place his mine at a strategic point, in darkness? He could then lead his cable under water and connect the mine, wiring the stolen cable to a dynamo exploder several hundred yards away? Hidden from the British while he observed the movement of ships, he could wait until the right moment, then use his dynamo exploder to fire the mine? Very well. Ruck Keene brandished his dividers, and indicated a wreck in the harbour. The saboteur could hide himself aboard such a wreck with his dynamo exploder. The distance from the wreck to the oiling wharf was less than nine hundred yards—and nine hundred yards of cable had been stolen.

Within twenty-four hours Ruck Keene's destroyers were due to go alongside the oiling wharf to refuel. If there was a mine under water on it, and if the mine was fired at the right time, it could create maximum alarm and despondency. Fired close enough to the destroyer's magazine to create a sympathetic explosion, the mine would destroy the destroyer and much of the harbour of Haifa. Ruck Keene stopped talking and looked at Crabb. 'Get your diving team together,' he said, 'and come back and report to me when you find the mine *on the oiling wharf.*'

The theory was plausible. It was a possible explanation for the theft of so much cable, but to Crabb, it appeared more appropriate to detective fiction than to anti-sabotage diving. The police had searched the wreck, but it was possible that the saboteur aboard her had hidden, then returned to his post. It would have been neither good-mannered nor wise of Crabb to communicate his doubts to Ruck Keene. 'Well, don't just sit there,' said the captain; 'go to the oiling wharf and get that mine. Don't jump up like a scalded cat, man. Finish your drink.'

Crabb joined the diving team of six petty officers in the diving-launch tied up alongside the *Chequers*. As the launch began its run towards the oiling wharf, he explained the theory to the petty officers. They were polite, well-disciplined men and they made no comment. The launch reached the oiling wharf and Crabb fitted his breathing-gear and took first dive. For the first time in his diving career, he was mortally afraid that a mine would *not* be there. And there was the mine. There were leads from it—the missing cable had also been found. He was so pleased to find that the captain was right that he swam towards the mine, until he remembered a significant detail and surfaced.

If the saboteurs were on watch, they would have seen him dive and they would know that the game was up. Nothing prevented them from detonating the mine while he was in the water. If he chose he could cut the cable immediately, risking a short-circuit which would cause the mine to explode, or he could assume that the saboteurs were not on watch and remove the mine with the cable still in place. 'Cutters,' he ordered, 'and get the launch out of the way the moment I'm over the side.'

He swam back and cut the cable quickly; the mine survived. He removed it from the wharf. Then, in turn, he and his petty officers went over the side, tracing the direction of the cable. The cable led back towards the wreck, but by the time they were certain of this the far end of the cable had been thrown over the side and the saboteurs had vanished with their dynamo exploder. As he swam back to the diving-launch for the last time, Crabb was aware of something on his thigh. He thought at first that his knife-belt was flapping, then he found that a sucker fish had attached itself to him and was hanging by its head to his skin. He took grave exception to being mistaken for a shark, and he had to brush the creature off six times before he reached the launch.

He boarded H.M.S. *Chequers* and reported to Captain D. 'Have you found it?' roared the captain. 'Jolly good. I knew it was there. How many divers have you got? Six? Bring them here.' He produced a bottle of whisky and some glasses for all but himself, explaining that he never drank before lunch-time. He particularly asked Crabb to drink up. Crabb, he said, had been high on a terrorist assassination list for some time. Nothing like enjoying the present, said Ruck Keene.

There were few such mornings in Haifa. For a year, life was both tedious and dangerous, like unending flight in an unsafe aeroplane. In the spring of 1947 Crabb was at last ordered home. At Malta, he went aboard Ruck Keene's ship to bid good-bye. 'What do you want?' the captain asked. 'Paying my respects on leaving station, sir.' Ruck Keene acknowledged this with a nod and continued pacing up and down. He said that there were two things on his mind. The first was his war gratuity. He had received the money *in a Post Office Savings book*. A post captain, of his seniority, at sea the whole war, was being insulted in such a fashion. If they had any money to give him, why couldn't they send it to his bank? The second thing was that the headlights of his brand-new car had been stolen in daylight in Valetta. When such matters troubled Ruck Keene, the war was clearly over.

Until then Crabb had not given too much thought to his intentions in peace-time. To think of England was to think of autumn and of walking in a light rain, with gentle subtle colouring all round, towards a pub. He had often thought of how pleasant it would be to stand with one elbow on a bar and listen to strangers talking, without having to guard his back. He anticipated walking into a phone booth, an odd experience in itself, putting two pennies in a slot, dialling the number of a girl he knew and saying, 'Hullo. Crabbie here.

167

Yes, I'm back. Look here, what about a meal or something?'

London was older and greyer than he had realised. Very few people whom he had known well were in town. He bumped into people whom he vaguely remembered and who vaguely remembered him. 'Hullo, Admiral. Haven't seen you for years. Been away?'

The more he saw of civilian life in London, the more enthusiastic he became about the Service. But the Navy was becoming steadily smaller and there was very little room for officers of the Volunteer Reserve. Crabb became engaged to be married, and found a house to rent in the green country. In the spring of 1948 he walked out of a demobilisation centre in Portsmouth with a cardboard box which held a grey chalk-stripe flannel suit. He hadn't the slightest idea of what sort of job he should try, other than a job in diving.

The wedding, after all, did not take place. He let the rented house go, and moved into the Cavendish Hotel in London. Rosa Lewis still owned the hotel, but now she was old and ill. Occasionally she recognised him when he passed and said in surprise, 'Hullo, Admiral. What are you doing here?'

Crabb's money was running low, but he believed there was a future in civilian life as a diver. What he had to do was to fill in with some sort of job until he could find his way back to the water. An old friend helped him to mark time by making him responsible for a variety of small printing and publishing contracts, and he set to work bringing out a sports writer's handbook of advice on how to win the football pools. He had no idea what the writer meant by words like 'permutation', and he was terrified the printers would ask him some technical question like 'What division is Chelsea in?'

Then the owner of a fleet of herring drifters contacted him; he talked of how the echo-sounders of fishery vessels picked up shoals of fish without being able to identify the size or formation of the shoal, or the type of fish. He wanted to know if it was possible, after the echo-sounders had made a strike, for a frogman to go down to observe the type of fish and their formation so that echo-sounding could be read more accurately. He also said that fishermen were divided in their opinion on how shoals of fish reacted when they encountered nets. If he could have first-hand information upon this, he could adjust his use of nets and vastly increase his haul.

The idea appealed to Crabb, and he sailed with a drifter fleet from Yarmouth in the herring moon of October 1948 to make a preliminary reconnaissance. He was able to report that it was a practical proposition. There was sufficient clarity of water for a team of shallow-water divers to go down, observe the size, type and formation of shoal, and to take moving pictures with 35-millimetre cameras of how the nets formed and how the shoal reacted.

He was given a variety of promises and told to stand by, but it became clear that the promises would take long to mature. He continued his printing and publishing side-line, sharing a one-roomed office high above Fleet Street, making a one-man stand against the paper shortage. It was a brave fight while it lasted, but the shortage won.

He had a great deal of spare time, and he spent much of it wondering why the country was so slow to appreciate the possibilities of shallow-water divers. Even the Customs authorities did not seem aware of them. It would be easy for underwater smugglers to clamp their wares in canisters to the bilge keels of ships at the port of departure, having arranged for the canisters to be removed by other underwater smugglers at the port of call. A very bulky canister of neutral buoyancy could be towed away in darkness without a ripple breaking the surface.

He wrote to the Customs authorities, drew their attention to the danger and suggested they should recruit ex-Naval shallow-water divers for underwater Customs checks. He could not see why a small, highly mobile team should not be employed to do surprise checks at various ports. He suggested, diffidently, that the team might possibly include himself. A reply signed by the Deputy Inspector General of Customs and Excise arrived promptly:

Dear Mr. Crabb,

I beg to acknowledge receipt of your letter of the 2nd inst. A further communication will be sent to you in due course, but you will no doubt realise that full consideration of your proposals may take some time.

Seven years later, when no further communication had arrived, he decided that his proposals were receiving full consideration indeed.

When a friend he had trusted borrowed £120 and paid with a bad cheque, Crabb touched rock-bottom. He was left heavily in debt to other friends who had trusted him. He went over his possessions, and there was not a lot that he could sell. Round his neck on a piece of fish-line he always wore a large piece of ornamental jade. The jade was almost the colour of the moon, a milky green. Before the war, in Singapore, the Chinaman who had tried to teach him Chinese had made him a present of it, and he had worn it as a talisman from that day. When he showed it to a dealer, it reflected light like a little moon in the hand. The dealer agreed that the jade was good, but times were hard, he said, and jade no longer seemed to interest people. These were times of austerity, the dealer went on, developing the theme. Just after the war there had been a lot of money around, but Service men had spent their gratuities, normal living was so expensive, and jade was a little . . . remote? One's clients, nowadays . . . He gave a sad, confiding smile and offered £7. Crabb nodded, he didn't feel like talking.

When this war is over
Oh, how happy we shall be . . .

171

But Crabb's luck was changing. His trip by trawler had reminded him of the possibilities of underwater photography. He called at the Admiralty Research Laboratory at Teddington and discovered how enormous the possibilities were. He was shown lengths of film taken by James Hodges, who had served in midget submarines on D Day and who, as a civilian, was experimenting with underwater cameras. The films showed a world under water which the public had never seen. Crabb had always found it difficult to recount what he had experienced, but here was a way of explaining things. He suggested that the films should be edited and worked upon and made into one film, perhaps by the Crown Film Unit. The Director of Boom Defence and Marine Salvage agreed. Crabb was asked to act as technical adviser, and in his Fleet Street office he also wrote the script for the film, which went out to the public as 'Wonders of the Deep'.

The Director of Boom Defence and Marine Salvage then offered him a job in underwater photography. He was seconded for work at the Admirality Research Laboratory at Teddington in the spring of 1949, to experiment with underwater photography and underwater lighting. With Jimmy Hodges he began to dive, to photograph wrecks in harbours, to help salvage divers before they began; to film the behaviour of underwater weapons and equipment; to experiment with new cameras, new lights, new breathing equipment, new diving-suits.

Much of the work was secret and important. Crabb was being paid, as he put it, 'as a sort of honorary civil servant'; but at the Admiralty Research Laboratory his deep-rooted suspicion of the Civil Service remained. He sometimes carried a sword-stick with a crab engraved on the handle; he explained that he carried it to help him about, since he was prematurely aged by his dealings with civil servants. He was very happy. He would not have complained about the Civil Service if he had not been happy. His remarks were always impersonal. The civil servants at Admiralty Research were delightful chaps in his opinion. Wasn't their fault, fault of the system.

In January of 1950 he began to prepare equipment for a foreign tour. In the Mediterranean a naval clearance-diving team was re-forming, and in the spring they were to do a lot of work at Malta. One of the jobs concerned the s.s. *Breconshire* which had been sunk in a war-time air raid. Around the *Breconshire* were a number of unexploded bombs which had to be removed before salvage divers went down. While clearance divers dealt with the bombs, Crabb was to swim round, filming the operation. Meantime he played poker by night and spent his days in happy preparation.

On Thursday, 12th January, his peace of mind was shattered by the 10 P.M. radio news bulletin.

CHAPTER 12

THE
"TRUCULENT"

Dusk came early on 12th January 1950, and then it was a particularly dark night.

In the estuary of the Thames, the Swedish motorship *Divina* took a pilot on board and sailed on with her cargo of paraffin for Purfleet. At 7:05 P.M. there was a crunching forward and the ship lost way with a jerk. The ship's floodlights were turned on, but there was no sign of the craft she had struck. Time passed before the captain of the *Divina* realised that the vessel he had sunk was not some small surface craft. He sent his ship up and down the dark water in a search for men; he could not contact the shore with his radio telephone.

The first officer of the Dutch steamer *Almdijk* heard shouting in the water above the sound of the steamer's

174

engines. A searchlight was switched on, the *Almdijk* sailed towards the shouting and her lights fell on five men struggling in the water. The skipper picked them up, had them attended to and made his first signal to the shore at 7:49, but he did not immediately realise the extent of the disaster. Not until 8:15 was the skipper able to talk to the survivors, and then he made the signal which set Operation Subsmash in motion: 'H.M. Submarine *Truculent* sunk north-west Red Sands Tower between X.4 buoy and E. Piles buoy. Believe submarine has been in collision with the Swedish ship *Divina*. All ships please keep a lookout.'

The position he gave was almost in mid-channel at the mouth of the Thames Estuary, seventeen miles north-west of Margate, between Whitstable and Foulness Island off the Essex coast. An hour and five minutes later the destroyer *Cowdray* passed Garrison Point, outward bound from Sheerness, and Operation Subsmash had begun. It was a magnificent effort for a ship under four hours' steaming notice.

At ten, when Crabb turned on his radio, he heard the first public announcement of the collision. The bulletin had very little detail. A Dutch steamer had picked up five survivors, including the *Truculent's* captain, who had been thrown clear from the bridge. The ship which had sunk the submarine had cruised up and down the area of collision, picking up eight survivors and two dead men. Two more men who had escaped from the submarine on the bottom had been recovered alive. Thus fifteen had been saved from a submarine with seventy-nine men. There must be men alive below.

Crabb sat for a few minutes while his mind tried to order the facts. The *Truculent* was lying in about sixty feet of water, well within a frogman's reach. Standard divers would try to get down to her, but a frogman with self-contained gear and with swimfins might reach the submarine much faster than a standard diver could. The tide in the Thames Estuary was so strong that standard divers would have to wait for slack water, when the tide was just on the turn. A frogman might not have to wait. Once down, he might be able to swim along the submarine, whereas a standard diver with his lines and heavy boots could, at best, walk, and would probably have to crawl. If there were still men alive aboard the *Truculent,* if their escape hatch had been fouled, every minute would count.

He rang the duty Commander at the Admiralty, volunteered his services, and was told to stand by. He rang the Admiralty Research Laboratory for permission to make the attempt. Jimmy Hodges, the other diver and cameraman at the Laboratory, also wanted to come, and he arranged to collect their gear at Teddington and to drive into London.

Before midnight their offer had been accepted and

they were off by road on the forty-eight-mile journey to Sheerness.

When they arrived there the distress buoy of the *Truculent* had not been sighted and her exact position was not known. Shortly after seven, the distress buoy should have gone up with a calcium flare which should have burned for half an hour to lead rescue craft towards her, but seven hours later it had still not been found. A Lancaster aircraft which was to carry divers to the search had crashed in its first minute of flight, killing all its crew.

When the *Divina* had transferred the eight survivors that she carried and began to come in, Crabb and Hodges went out on a tug to board her. They hoped to learn something from her which could help them when they dived. On the way out they snatched half an hour's sleep. It proved a pointless journey. At the *Divina's* waterline was a tangle of metal from the deck casing or outer shell of the submarine, which told them nothing. The captain and pilot could add no details to what was already known. They were weary and numb and there was little to be gained from questioning them.

When the *Divina* came into Sheerness, the submarine's distress buoy had still not been sighted, and somebody suggested breakfast.

Then a rescue vessel picked up the *Truculent's* buoy in her searchlights and signalled the shore. The divers were told to make best speed to a fast motor-boat which was waiting for them. When they had gathered their gear and reached the boat, they found it loaded with reporters and photographers who refused to get out. There was a nightmarish quality about the whole situation. Crabb and Hodges tried to explain that they needed the boat to make the first attempt to get down to the *Truculent*.

The men in the boat replied that they had been promised the first boat out and that there was room for all of them. The divers explained that there was no such thing, the boat was hardly large enough for them to spread and prepare their gear. There was not space for a single passenger.

Crabb appreciated that petty officials with petty minds never have time to help or to talk to the Press. Only senior officers and men in important jobs can find the time. Under other circumstances he would have been glad to help, but at this moment he happened to be very busy. The men in the boat answered that they had been bothered about all night. Every man they had tried to interview had proved to be the one man who was saving the men from the *Truculent* and who was too busy to help them. This was the first boat out; they had been promised it, they were on it and they were staying on it. The assistant captain of the dockyard came along and cleared the craft.

The motor-boat turned out and sped towards the frigate standing by the buoy, while the divers got into their rubber suits. They boarded the frigate to confer quickly with the submarine staff officers waiting for them. Only when the divers were briefed did they appreciate how bad the situation was.

The survivors who had escaped from within the submarine were suffering from exposure, and all of them had been affected by oil in the eyes. The accounts they had given rescuers were not full accounts, but they certainly suggested catastrophe. The *Truculent* had been struck by the *Divina* as she dived in an attempt to avoid the motor-ship. She had flooded fast and found bottom in the silt, in sixty feet of water. Between thirty and forty men had gathered in the unflooded aft compartments of the submarine, watertight doors had been closed, and the marker buoy with its calcium flare had gone up to the surface before 7.10 P.M. The First Lieutenant of the *Truculent* had prepared to organise escape through the engine-room escape hatch. He had decided that since there was not enough air in the aft compartments for all of them, he could not afford to wait until light to make the escape, or even allow very long for rescue craft to gather. In any case, all the men in the aft compartments could hear propellors overhead, and assumed that they had been located.

Escape apparatus had been lost in the flooded compartments of the submarine; insufficient DSEA sets remained for all the men. The sets were given to the weaker swimmers, and controlled flooding-up began to

179

allow the escape hatch to be opened. All the men in
the aft compartments had gone out. When they reached
the surface, there had been lights and shouts and the
dark shape of the *Divina,* zigzagging up and down in
her search. But the *Divina* could not see them. All
but ten of the men, having survived the crash and the
dive in the fast-flooding submarine, having escaped
from the submarine and reached the surface, had gone
racing seawards on the tide, drowning or dying of
exposure in the dark between ships in the busiest river
estuary in the world.

There might be men still alive and trapped in the
Truculent, in the control-room beneath the conning
tower—if they had managed to close the hatch in time.
To reach them Crabb and Hodges would have to anchor
their boat right over the submarine. But the tide was
running at a full three knots. With a tide of such force,
they dared not risk using the distress buoy and its
slender wire to the submarine as a mooring; the strain
would be too great. If the wire snapped and the buoy
were set adrift, the last chance of a quick dive to the
Truculent would be lost. The only way they could
attempt to moor was by cruising over the submarine
with the motor-boat's anchor trailing until the anchor
fouled in the superstructure of the *Truculent.*

As they made the first run in with the anchor trailing,
a second boat, coming up suddenly, almost cut across
them. The civilians in the boat were so anxious to get

close to the *Truculent's* distress buoy that they endangered the drift of the anchor. Then they were almost on the buoy itself. If the sightseers fouled the marker wire of the distress buoy, the buoy would certainly be set adrift. Just as suddenly, the boat sheered off. In the diving-boat the coxswain tried again, began his second run with the anchor trailing, and managed to hook it in the periscope standard of the *Truculent*.

The boat rocked, the anchor held, the cable took the strain.

At a twenty-degree angle, the anchor cable stretched taut through the black race of water to the submarine below. There was no question of 'diving', or of swimming, in such a tide. The only way down was to grab the taut slant of cable and then go down the cable, hand over hand, working the swimfins to keep balance and to reduce the strain as the body was swept back by the force of water. Neither Crabb nor Hodges had ever tried before to go down a wet slant of cable against a three-knot tide. The water was dirt dark, quite black two feet beneath the surface. They had a small sodium lamp with a portable generator, but the generator would not start.

Crabb dived for the anchor cable and began to fight his way down. Once below, he could not see the cable. He was swept back holding on by one hand. When he was beaten, he got back to the boat; Hodges tried with the same resolution and also failed. In the diving-

boat they tried to discuss the problem, but planes dropping to a hundred feet over the buoy made it impossible
for one to hear what the other said. Within half an
hour there would be a slackening in the tide. Meantime
they vented their anger on the generator of the sodium
lamp.

An ordinary underwater light would only have been
blanketed by the scatter of the very dirty water, merely
thrown back at the divers as a car drivers headlights
are thrown back by fog. But the orange light of the
sodium lamp might not be entirely affected. When a
salvage officer came on board their boat and persuaded
the generator to start, Crabb and Hodges grew more
cheerful. Over the side of the launch went a weighted
shot rope, with a half-hundredweight sink an the end.
The sink found bottom by the side of the *Truculent*,
and so they had a second rope down.

When the tide slackened to a knot and a half, Hodges
went down the shot rope and Crabb went down the
anchor cable with the lamp. There were bad moments,
with one hand off the cable in the traverse, when the
water dragged his body back and out of line, but nearer
the bed the current slackened and Crabb knew that he
would get down. He reached the periscope standard
and at last stood on the bridge of the *Truculent*.

It was pitch black, every step stirred up the silt, the
sodium lamp gave, at most, a foot of visibility, no more
than a friendly glow. There was no immediate impact

182

of a sunken submarine on the eye or on the mind. He felt his way to the outside of the control-room and began to tap. He tapped on, but there was no response.

He was aware of the horror of the metal coffin in the silt, then the horror passed. He had to work his way aft to the engine-room escape hatch and there join up with Hodges. They were to try together to get back through the twill trunk of the escape hatch into the submarine. He had to clear his mind, he had to concentrate.

From the periscope standards of a submarine, a jumping-wire runs fore and aft to the bows and to the stern. With the periscope and radar aerials down, the wire is the highest thing on the submarine and normally helps her to slide under nets. Crabb chose to go astern by pulling himself along the jumping-wire of the *Truculent*, partly to ensure that the lead from his lamp to the surface would not foul on sharp edges. It did not occur to him that the jumping-wire was covered in grease.

He found Hodges at the engine-room escape hatch examining the twill trunk from the hatch. It was fouled, caught up inside the submarine, like a twisted trouser-leg. It was then that Crabb realised that he was running out of air. He had two air-bottles, one on either hip. From force of habit he closed the valve of the first, almost empty, air-bottle with his left hand before he reached round with his right to open the valve of the second bottle.

His right hand, covered with grease from the jumping-wire he had traversed, slid round and round the second valve. Twice he thought he had enough purchase to crack it open, then his fingers went sliding on. With his left hand he tried to open the valve of the almost empty bottle which he had just closed. There might be just enough air left in the first bottle to take him to the surface. The fingers of his left hand slid on the valve. It had been easily closed, but now it refused to open.

His companion, quite unaware of all this, was still trying to straighten the twist in the escape trunk.

Crabb had no chance of making the surface alive without opening one of the valves. The surface was about fifty feet away, through the current and the dark. The shot rope was out of reach. He had the lead from his sodium lamp as his only guide to the boat, up there in the air and the daylight. Aboard the launch, the crew saw the lamp lead tighten as it was tugged. Assuming that the diver wanted a longer lead, they slackened off the cable.

Crabb felt it slacken, and still he tried to get up, using it as a guide. Anything to get up to the daylight— he was making the attempt instinctively. He kept his right hand on the cable, while his left went sliding round the valve of the almost empty bottle of air as he made a last effort to open it. Suddenly the valve opened, and there was enough air to take him back to the surface.

Hodges joined him later in the diving-boat.

'Trouble?' he asked.

'Well . . . I thought I was at a dead stop for breathing. Bit of a flap.'

Hodges began to question him.

'Can't hear a bloody thing for the planes,' Crabb said.

When he felt a little better, they had a conference. The escape-hatch trunk was twisted and it was beyond them to straighten it to get inside the submarine. Having established beyond all doubt that all survivors had left the *Truculent*, they reported what they had found and were thanked for their work. Their job was over. Soon standard divers would be able to descend and make a detailed examination of the hull. They went aboard a bar vessel to change very slowly, drained by fatigue and by frustration.

There was a photographer at Crabb's elbow. He had climbed aboard the bar vessel and come up quietly from behind. He wanted a photograph of Crabb and Hodges, standing by the flag. The photographer's mate, meantime, was preparing the job. He was bringing the White Ensign down to half mast.

The Southend lifeboat came in after a search for forty miles out to sea; the Margate lifeboat returned to its base after fifteen hours; H.M.S. *Zest* brought six

185

bodies from Barrow Deep. H.M.S. *Cowdray* berthed with the ten survivors from within the submarine, and later that day some of the survivors were able to talk of the night before.

At 7.40 the escape hatch had been ready for use. The men had queued in an orderly fashion; they were short of air but they had laughed and joked. One survivor said that it had all been so smoothly organised that it was like waiting for a bus. Lieutenant Hindes, the First Lieutenant, was completely calm. His orders were clear. He knew that when he opened up the way for the men to escape he might be pulled out violently with the escaping air. He told a man to hold his feet, but he was pulled out of the submarine to die. The sense of order that he had instilled survived him.

Electrical Assistant Edward Buckingham said that the last man out of the escape hatch was Chief Engine Room Artificer Hime. Hime had taken over the escape arrangements when Lieutenant Hindes was lost. Buckingham himself had been last but one, and he remembered the Chief telling him to go ahead.

By six P.M. on 13th January it was certain that no more survivors would be found. The searching planes flew back to their stations and the ships came back to their ports.

CHAPTER 13

RE-ENTER
KNOWLES

In the early spring of 1950, a Royal Navy clearance-diving team set off on a training exercise to search for a galleon of the Spanish Armada, lying under silt in the Bay of Tobermory, Isle of Mull. The team included Leading Stoker Sydney James Knowles, B.E.M., and when Crabb joined the team in Tobermory, Crabb and Knowles had a touching reunion.

'Hullo, sir,' said Knowles.

'Hullo, Knowles,' said Crabb.

In conventional shallow-water diving-suits, Knowles and his comrades descended to the bed of the Bay and searched with pressure probes for the galleon, which was still between twenty and thirty feet below them, covered by the silt-carrying tides of centuries. Crabb, in self-contained gear, swam round the divers, assisting, encouraging, clearing obstructions. As Knowles put it, 'He came up at us, shouting, as if he was Hans Haas and we were sharks.'

At last, hard timber was located and the divers worked round the spot until they had charted what was considered to be the after end of the galleon. They came upon dagger sheaths and a fragment of African oak, oak which had been growing within fifty years of the Armada setting sail, oak which might well have timbered a galleon.

But in the fifty-seven days of work in locating and attempting to establish the identity of the wreck, wind and weather permitted diving on only seventeen days. When they could stay no longer, the naval clearance-diving team sailed away.

Four years passed. Crabb was recalled to the Navy, took part in the search for the lost submarine *Affray*, and was promoted to commander's rank. Meantime, Knowles left the Navy. Then in August of 1954 they returned to Tobermory. Crabb was on unpaid leave from the Navy, Knowles was on holiday from his job, and they were involved in a civilian attempt to reach the galleon. Crabb had been asked to lead the civilian divers; he had chosen Knowles and there were three other divers.

Working in shifts, sixty feet below the surface of

the Bay, the divers controlled the action of an airlift which sucked clay from the galleon, functioning like a gigantic vacuum-cleaner. By the beginning of October a deep shaft had been sunk in the clay, but the party was troubled by the size and quantity of stones they found over the galleon, stones from six inches to three feet across.

The airlift was for ever sucking at a stony sea and the work was seriously affected. Unprepared for the stones, the party had neither grabs for work in such deep water nor the means of acquiring such grabs. Aware of the danger of the stones, but unwilling to admit defeat, the party worked on.

It fell to Knowles to discover how great the danger was. He was working seventy-eight feet below the surface in a deep hole, facing a solid wall of clay, when a boulder tumbled from behind him, threw him on his face and held him down, while the clay which the boulder had dislodged covered him. He was buried for almost half an hour while Terry Yettan, the stand-by diver, struggled to get the boulder from his back, then to drag him clear of the clay.

All through the rescue operation his wife was on board the depot ship. Joan Knowles was not told of what was happening below, and when her husband was brought on board she was in the galley. When he joined her, she noticed that his face was tired and drawn. 'I think I've got a cold coming on,' he said.

Without grabs to clear the stones, there was no longer much point in attempting to work right through the winter as they had originally intended. The attempt to reach the galleon was over. On the day they were due to leave Tobermory, Crabb and Knowles went over the side to clear a trawler's screw, fouled by a tangle of wire. They had a certain amount of difficulty when the trawler's anchor dragged, when they drifted below in the tangle of wire towards some rocks. But they got on board and, as the trawler firmly re-anchored, Knowles said casually to Crabb "A near do was that, sir". They both grinned. Knowles had used that expression, in time of trouble, on and off for the past eleven years. They went over the side again to finish the job. Winter was coming to Mull on the Smirr from the sea. Crabb and Knowles were diving together for the last time.

CHAPTER 14

LAST DIVE

WHEN HE returned to London, Crabb had bad news. A letter from the Admiralty ended with this: 'Because of the present general position . . . there is no possibility of your being asked to extend your naval service beyond the current period.' As a reserve officer he would have no pension. Diving for the Navy was all that he wanted to do; he had neither the desire nor the training to follow any other trade. But he decided to put off the thought of the future as he reported to H.M.S. Vernon, the Underwater Countermeasures and Weapons Establishment, at Portsmouth for his last few months on service. He had no hard feelings toward the Navy. As he saw it, the decision to beach him and people like him had been made by Civil Servants. Pack of idiots, he said,

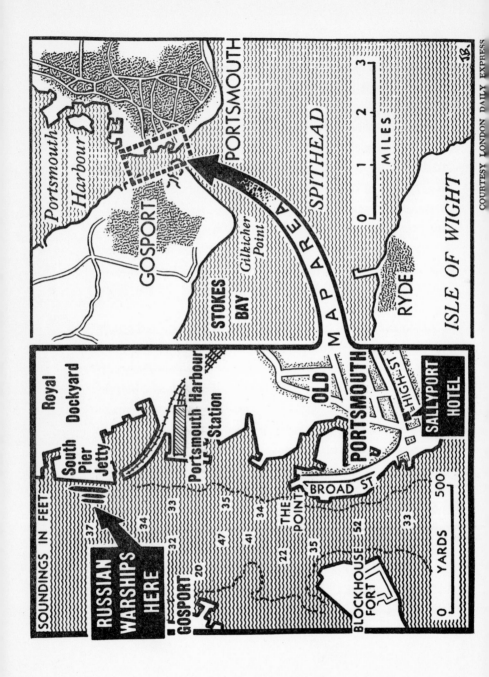

SOUNDINGS IN FEET

Royal
Dockyard

South
Pier
Jetty

RUSSIAN
WARSHIPS
HERE

37

32 33

34

47 35

41 34

22 THE POINT

35

GOSPORT

20

BLOCKHOUSE
FORT

52

33

Portsmouth Harbour
Station

BROAD ST

PORTSMOUTH

HIGH ST

OLD

SALLYPORT
HOTEL

0   500
YARDS

Portsmouth
Harbour

GOSPORT

STOKES
BAY

Gilkicher
Point

PORTSMOUTH

SPITHEAD

OLD MAP AREA

RYDE

ISLE OF WIGHT

0   1   2   3
MILES

fighting total paper warfare. . . . half a mind to write to them about it, using a quill to remind them of more gracious times. Hah!

In the second fortnight of December, a dredger at Portland brought up a massive metal object from the mud. Taking it for a torpedo warhead, the captain of the dredger informed the Navy and a torpedo officer was sent. He had one look at the 'warhead' before he cleared the area and made a signal requesting the immediate presence of a senior mine disposal officer. The object was a damaged mine which had been roughly handled and which might have been further affected by its shaking from the dredger's buckets.

As Crabb drove down from Portsmouth, he reflected on how often his nastier jobs had turned up at Christmas time. Although the mine was in a delicate state, it defied all his efforts to open it. From a distance, junior mine disposal men watched him set about the mine in his old, free style and they gained some of his confidence as the mine remained intact. Eventually he had to take it out to sea and blow it up with a remotely controlled charge. Some of his juniors concluded that their job was safer than they'd thought and he hoped they would never have reason to change their minds.

It was his last mine. His recall to the Navy ended in March 1955. The wives of most of his friends nagged him to settle down. He found a hotel room in Knightsbridge, tossed his brass hat on top of the wardrobe and relaxed. Once his leave was over he had every intention of looking for a steady job. Perhaps he would find a small right wing navy to train in underwater work, perhaps he would get in touch with a brewer and find himself an inn.

Meantime, we began to work on this book and, to Crabb's delight, part of the job was to contact his old colleagues and some of the Italians who had been technically his enemies in time of war. He had never lost touch with the Italians. Belloni was still bombarding him with blueprints of underwater inventions and three of the Belloni children had called on him, during a hitch-hiking tour of Britain. The submariner Borghese, had looked him up in London to thank him for the way he had handled Italian prisoners and to compliment him on the clean, hard war that he had fought. Of all the Italians at Sant' Andrea only the sergeants Fraguglia and Berni could not be traced. They had vanished and it was generally assumed that they had found themselves a little war.

The publishers sent a contract dated the 13th and Crabb sent it back, unsigned. He had dived to the *Truculent* on Friday, 13th, 1950; his marriage which lasted for a year had finally broken up on April 13th, 1953; the ill-fated expedition to Tobermory had set sail on Friday 13th August, 1954. The commander was enjoying himself working on a book and he declared that he would not have things spoiled by a contract with such a date. Knowles fully agreed. Having become a long-distance lorry driver on the Preston to London run, Knowles dropped in regularly to help us out. Discipline was maintained. Crabb beat Knowles decisively in several games of Lilliput football in a local bar.

Of the other members of the Underwater Working Party, Lieutenant Bailey was in Portugal, Morgan had died, Frazer could not be traced and Thomas—the diver who could not swim—had last been heard of applying for a job in the Swansea Fire Brigade. But Petty Officer Bell assisted and so did Chief Petty Officer Thorpe. As always, the Chief's memories were precise and accurate. He ended his contribution with "Well, I enjoyed every minute of it and we're still alive to tell the tale."

These were happy months for Crabb; he seemed completely at ease while he told anecdotes of Belloni, or played with my daughter and a helicopter he had bought for their joint amusement, or spent a quiet hour with 'God's Butlers', which was his affectionate phrase for the priests of Brompton Oratory in Knightsbridge. There, occasionally, he would light a candle and offer a prayer for his future and he was fairly certain that 'something will turn up. . . . things always work out right in the end.'

By way of a diversion, he began to argue about politics and the state of England or, as he phrased it 'to give those Socialists ten minutes hell'. He found difficulty in sustaining an argument for when he entered a room and began, without ceremony, to state that England was going to the dogs because of the trade unions and the disgusting standards of work in this country, Socialists would look for the mischievous glint in his eye, then grin. He had very many friends and, so far as I know, no enemies. Typically he had many friends in journalism for all his remarks on 'the Gutter Press'.

But when the first draft of the book was finished, time was somewhat heavy on his hands. He contacted a man who found employment for those over forty without result. Then he bought a bowler for an important interview, prepared for the interview with care, to discover that the young man who interviewed him had no particular interest in his future. Sometimes he thought of signing on as an able seaman on a merchant ship. 'Trouble is' he said to me 'have to join the Seamen's Union. Can't stand unions.' Then he cheered up and gave his deep, abrupt laugh as he remembered sailing as a merchant seaman gunner on one of the first convoys of the war. Even then he had refused to join the Union and the crew had considered having his gunnery declared 'black'.

The more uncertain his future in civilian life became, the more determined he was to get back into underwater work or, as he put it 'to get m' feet wet again, get m' gills back.'

Lt. Commander Bathurst, with whom Crabb had served in the search for the lost submarine *Affray*, had joined the Royal Canadian Navy, and he felt that Crabb was suited for a pending appointment in that Service. Much as he wanted the job, Crabb knew that he would have to drop back to lieutenant commander's rank for the appointment and he felt that to go to a junior service, in a lower rank, would 'let the Royal Navy down'. Bathurst argued the point; for night after night we continued the argument, but Crabb had made up his mind.

It was sometimes put to him that he was too old, too tired by his past exertions, too far out of training to take on arduous underwater work but he continued to hold that a good diver could go on until he was over fifty; continued to distrust training for training's sake; continued to believe that, in an emergency, the reserves 'don't come from the body. . . . . they come from some sort of spiritual stimulation' as he frequently said.

Occasionally he would set off on an outing for Portsmouth and be unusually vague about his intentions. For his Portsmouth trips, he had an almost ceremonial rig; fawn tweed suit, pork pie hat and the swordstick which had become something of a talisman after he had been forced to part with his piece of jade. In Portsmouth there was also an almost ceremonial joke. The naval diving friends who suspected that he had arrived on mysterious business would say "Hullo, Crabbie. Something on?"

197

And he would reply "Just dropped down for a haircut and a shave."

Once one of his old colleagues suggested that I should help persuade him to "stop this underwater business. He's done enough in his time." I did not know what the 'underwater business was' and, by his gentle evasions, Crabb made it clear that it was no business of mine. The thought of Naval Intelligence work did not occur to me and I attached no particular significance to the fact that, in Coronation Year, Crabb had done some unusual underwater job in the Canal Zone and, on return to England, had reported immediately to Lord Louis Mountbatten.

Just before Christmas, 1955, Crabb's luck appeared to change. Provision was to be made for a Western naval officer to advise the Iraqui Navy in underwater work and Crabb was privately informed that he had a very good chance of the job. While he waited, he began to work for an old acquaintance, as office manager of a concern which specialised in furnishings for espresso coffee bars. To his friend's amusement, the commander became heavily involved in the arrangements for a new espresso called 'Two Bare Feet'.

There followed a change in the political situation in the Middle East, with no immediate likelihood of any Western naval officer being called upon to advise the Iraqui Navy. Crabb said very little about this crushing disappointment. Occupying his mind with new espresso

tables and do-it-yourself furniture, he began to find
that his work took all of his time from nine in the morning until ten at night, six days a week. Then one night
he mentioned that he might want to borrow my car
for 'a little job down in Portsmouth about the middle
of April'. He seemed particularly brisk and cheerful.
I did not see him again.

At the time of writing this, there is very little on
Crabb's last movements and his last dive which can
be established with absolute certainty. Even in Parlia-
ment, a number of members—particularly those who
were loud in their condemnation of the irresponsible
Press—strayed rather far from the facts. Here I can
only give what I know myself and the statements made
by people in a position to know something of the affair.

Throughout his career, Crabb had a particular dislike
of writing letters. In the Navy unimportant signals
would sometimes be left, unanswered, pinned to his
desk by a bayonet. Before he paid his last visit to Portsmouth, he wrote to Petty Officer David Bell and said
how much he had enjoyed Bell's recent visit. He wrote
to the publishers; he wrote to his mother and said that
he was going on a 'little job' which would prove simple,
asked her not to worry and to tear up his letter.

It has been said that he was worrying about the job
ahead of him and not sleeping too well at nights. Some
little time before, he had sold two coffee tables to a Mr.
Bernard S. Smith, whose cheque in payment was

wrongly made out, the year given as 1955. An associate of Crabb's seems to have reason to believe that Smith and Crabb had worked together in the past on military intelligence work. Certainly Crabb pocketed Smith's cheque and said that he would have him alter it, when he met him in Portsmouth. The associate also believes that, just before Crabb left for Portsmouth, someone made a remark about 'looking at the Russians' bottom.' Since Crabb's disappearance a number of officers in shallow water diving have said that Crabb secretly examined the Russian cruiser Sverdlov when she called on Portsmouth in October, 1955.

In the middle of April, 1956, the Russian cruiser Ordzhonikidze, with two attendant destroyers, docked in Portsmouth, bringing Marshal Bulganin and Mr. Kruschev to Britain. Commander Crabb reached Portsmouth on Tuesday, April 17th and, with a tall, fair-haired man of about forty, known as Mr. Smith, booked into the Sallyport Hotel. He had arranged to keep in touch with the office in London and, on Wednesday evening, he phoned and is reported to have said "Well, I'm not as old as I thought." At the time, his associates believed that he was talking of a medical examination, for he'd been having trouble with his eyes and his ears. Later they believed that he had meant that he felt confident, having had a practice swim.

Later on the same evening of April 18th, he had a re-union meeting with a petty officer and a lieutenant

commander, and the lieutenant commander's wife.
There was no talk of Crabb diving, although the other
officer was one of Crabb's most valued friends. He did
not have diving gear in his room at the Sallyport Hotel.
He had a key and the hotel keeper is uncertain of when
he returned from his meeting with friends or when he
finally left on April 19.

When time passed without any call from Portsmouth
Crabb's employer phoned the Sallyport Hotel, to learn
that Mr. Smith had returned to the hotel to pay both
bills and had collected Crabb's belongings. At last the
employer contacted the lieutenant commander who had
been with Crabb on the evening of April 18 and who
had arranged to meet him again on April 20. When this
officer began to make discreet enquiries, he was ordered
to say nothing more of the affair and to refrain from
ringing Crabb's employer.

Six days after the commander had vanished, a naval
captain called at the Espresso furnishing business and
asked the employer to come to his flat. There the captain
said that Commander Crabb had disappeared on underwater tests in the Portsmouth area, during the previous
week. He advised Crabb's employer not to talk about
it and he asked him for the address of Crabb's mother,
his next of kin. Naval records, he explained, still carried
the name of Crabb's former wife as his next of kin.

On the following day I rang the secretary of the
Deputy Chief of Naval Staff and pointed out that Com-

mander Crabb had many friends in journalism and that the manner in which the affair was being handled seemed more likely to provoke publicity than to prevent it. Later in the day, the captain who had called on Crabb's employer asked me to his flat. He repeated the general statement that Crabb was missing, added that 'they' did not know exactly what had happened to him but that there was always a possibility that he might have been picked up by a trawler. Seven days had passed since Crabb, a weak swimmer, had disappeared. The possibility of him being picked up by a trawler did not strike me as particularly likely. The captain agreed and said that it seemed most probable that Crabb was dead.

An Admiralty announcement was to be made, once Crabb's mother had been informed. On Friday, April 27th, the captain rang me to say that he had seen Crabb's mother and would see his former wife on the following day. He added that no statement would, after all, be issued by the Admiralty but that a statement was now *available* at the Admiralty, should any journalist enquire. I had already made the point to him that reporters would find the approximate date and place of Crabb's disappearance very interesting, but he had made no comment.

On Sunday, April 29th, I informed the newspapers that a statement would be available at the Admiralty. The captain later told me that he intended me to do so.

When reporters phoned the Admiralty, their curiosity was aroused, first by the wording of the statement. Commander Crabb was presumed dead (not missing) after failing to return from a test dive which took place in connection with the trials of certain underwater apparatus, in the Portsmouth area, about a week before. Some time during the afternoon, the words 'in Stokes Bay' were added to the Admiralty statement. The phrase had not occurred in the original statement which the Resident Clerk made to me. Stokes Bay is some three miles from the berth at which the Russian cruiser was lying; an impossible distance for Crabb to swim. Later, when the naval correspondent of the *Times* asked to see the original statement, he was told that it was no longer available.

The following day, someone who should have known of all naval underwater activities in the Portsmouth area rang me to ask what I knew of the affair. He said that he had known nothing of Crabb's disappearance until he saw it in the newspapers and that, so far as he knew, the commander had neither drawn equipment from, nor worked through the Navy at Portsmouth. Meantime, at least four reporters had discovered that Crabb had been staying with Mr. Smith at the Sallyport Hotel. This did not strike them as significant until a detective superintendent of Portsmouth police had four pages removed from the hotel register. Asked to comment, a police spokesman in Portsmouth mentioned the Official Secrets Act. This action further alerted the newspapers which were already making enquiries. It also greatly interested the *Times* which at first had been inclined to accept the Admiralty statement as it stood.

On the day the hotel register action was reported, a question was tabled in the House of Commons and on the following day, an assistant naval attaché at the Soviet Embassy in London was reported to have said that a frogman had been seen from the Russian cruiser Ordzhonikidze, in Portsmouth Harbour.

By this time, some of Crabb's former colleagues who had not been officially advised on how they should act, were making enquiries of their own. Their theory, based on their findings, experience and knowledge was this: He had been working for a military or naval intelligence group and he had been sent to examine the hull of the Russian cruiser, or those of the attendant destroyers, as they believed he had examined the Sverdlov, some six months before. He would have been wearing oxygen breathing gear so that no bubbles would be seen. During the operation, he would have to dive below 33 feet, the maximum depth at which oxygen breathing gear is considered to be safe. The officers' enquiries led them to believe that Crabb, full well aware of the risk, had dived alone and had, most probably, contracted oxygen poisoning. He had been taking chances, especially with the gear he wore, ever since his first days in Gibraltar.

With the passage of years, he had become progressively less willing to allow others to take the risks he took himself. As they saw it, Crabb would be prepared to dive alone but that it was up to the officials who had arranged the job to have ensured that he had a second diver. On all normal underwater work Naval divers are not allowed to take such a risk alone.

On May 4th, the Prime Minister, Sir Anthony Eden, said in the House of Commons that "It would not be in the public interest to disclose the circumstances in which Commander Crabb is presumed to have met his death. While it is the practice for Ministers to accept responsibility, I think it is necessary in the special circumstances of this case, to make it clear that what was done was done without the authority or the knowledge of her Majesty's Ministers. Appropriate disciplinary steps are being taken."

Mr. Hugh Gaitskell, Leader of the Opposition asked "Are you aware that, while we would all wish to protect public security, the suspicion must inevitably arise that your refusal to make a statement on this subject is not so much in the interests of public security but to hide a very grave blunder?"

It was by then being generally assumed that Commander Crabb had died on service. When Commander Crabb's personal effects, taken from the Sallyport Hotel by Mr. Bernard Smith, were returned to Crabb's mother by the naval captain who had first informed her that

her son was missing, many believed that the link between Mr. Smith and the Navy had been more clearly
established.

Two days after the Prime Minister's statement, Mos-
cow Radio broadcast the texts of Notes exchanged by
the Soviet and British Governments. According to the
Soviet Note, a frogman had been observed floating
between the Soviet destroyers at 7.30 a.m. on the morning of April 19. The commanding officer of the Russian
ships had mentioned the matter to the Chief of Staff
at Portsmouth who had categorically rejected the possibility. "In fact, however, as it transpired from reports
published in the British press on April 30", the Note
went on, "the fact that the British naval authorities had
carried out secret underwater tests in the area where
the Soviet warships were anchored at Portsmouth was
confirmed. Moreover, the carrying out of these tests
resulted in the death of the British frogman."

The British Note in reply stated that "the diver seen
to be swimming between the Soviet destroyers was, to
all appearances, Commander Crabb and that his presence in the vicinity of the destroyers occurred without
any permission whatever." Regret for the incident was
expressed.

Then the commanding officer of the Russian ships
involved gave an interview to *Pravda* in which he said
that the statement that Crabb's presence close to the
Russian's warships occurred without permission was by

no means convincing' and speculation continued throughout the world.

Who, it was asked, had issued the order? What was Crabb attempting to find out? Had he been recovered, dead or alive, by the Russians or by his own colleagues? Had he been killed by an anti-frogman device on the Russian ships? Why had no attempt been made to recover a body which might have been trapped in a known area of the harbour by debris or by the very weight of the diving gear? Why had a number of statements independently made by private individuals in London and Portsmouth suggested that Commander Crabb was alive and on land in Portsmouth, some hours after 7:30 A.M., the time given in the Russian note?

On May 14th, the case of Commander Crabb was debated in the House of Commons. In his opening remarks Mr. Hugh Gaitskell, Leader of the Opposition, said "Whatever may be the circumstances in which he met his death, all of us will agree that this country would be the poorer if it were not for men like Commander Crabb." In his examination of the case Mr. Gaitskell said that he would have to conclude that "presumably the Secret Service or a secret service and the Admiralty must have been mixed up in the plan from the start."

The Prime Minister was not prepared to add to his original statement and he said "The national interest is of first importance to us in the House of Commons,

207

but there is also a very important international interest, and I confess that all I care for is that the outcome of our discussions with the Soviet leaders should in truth prove to be, as I have said, the beginning of a beginning. . . . I deplore this debate and I will say no more."

The debate ran for an hour and thirty eight minutes and, whatever else it may have achieved, disclosed nothing about the last dive of Commander Crabb.